PEOPLE'S WAR AND AFTERMATH NEPAL: THE ROLE OF TRUTH AND RECONCILIATION COMMISSION

.

PEOPLE'S WAR AND AFTERMATH NEPAL: THE ROLE OF TRUTH AND RECONCILIATION COMMISSION

(With Case Studies of Liberia, Sierra Leone and South Africa)

Sunil Thapa

&

Dr Drew Cottle

Vij Books India Pvt Ltd

New Delhi (India)

Designed and Setting by

Vij Books India Pvt Ltd
2/19, Ansari Road, Darya Ganj,
New Delhi - 110002 (India)
www.vijbooks.com

Dedication

To all the Nepalis who suffered directly and/or indirectly from the People's War.

Table of Contents

Foreword

Given the civil unrest that has been predominant throughout Nepal, particularly during the "People's War" (1996-2006), this book on the aftermath and interventions by the Truth and Reconciliation Commission (Nepal) is timely. While the debate over the Nepali Constitution and the role of government continues, it is important to gain an objective understanding of the events, struggles and injustices visited upon Nepali citizens during their nation's time of crisis. In contemporary times there has been mounting attention paid to mass cruelties such as widespread extermination, illegalities of war, crimes against humankind and other uncivilized human rights defilements. Simultaneously, there has been a considerable progression in the number of scholars and academics seeking to suggest the origins of, and submit pragmatic resolutions to, these barbarisms. Yet there continues to be the deficient dialogue about the realistic and moral questions encompassing research into severe maltreatment of individuals and dealing with susceptible populations.

This book brings together case studies from three African nations, taking a strong and often times challenging stance on the causes and consequences on each of their civil wars, functions of their Truth and Reconciliation Commissions; and a comparison of the strengths and weaknesses of each of their Truth and Reconciliation Commissions. With the United Nations establishment of "Rule of Law Tools for the Post-Conflict States: Truth Commissions", a way forward for each of these countries was attained. In the case of Nepal, the slow establishment and slow functioning of their Truth and Reconciliation Commission, mandates, progress till date, and criticisms regarding slow functioning, are examined. These comprehensive chapters provide insights into the final chapter, where recommendations are made to the Nepali Truth and Reconciliation

Commission, emanating from the study of the of three African nations' cases for the establishment of peace. This book addresses the human rights violations committed in Nepal and provides a way forward for victims as well as perpetrators; and suggests ways in which they can move forward together.

Best wishes and congratulations to the authors.

– Dr Wendy Hillman PhD, MSocSc, GCE (TT), BA (Hons)
Central Queensland University, Australia

List of Acronyms

ACC	Anti-corruption Commission
ACS	American colonization society
AFRC	Armed Forces Ruling Council
AMMAA	Agreement on Monitoring of the Management of Arms and Armies
ANC	African national congress
APC	All People's Congress
ASOFAMD	Association of Relatives of the Disappeared Detainees and Martyrs for National Liberation of Bolivia
CA	Constitution assembly
CED	Commission on enforced disappearances
CEDAW	Elimination of All Forms of Discrimination against Women
CIEPD	Commission of investigation on enforced disappeared persons
COID	Commission on Investigation of Disappeared Persons
CPA	Comprehensive peace accord/ comprehensive peace agreement
CPN (M)	Communist Party of Nepal (Maoist)
CPNUML	Communist Party of Nepal -United Marxist and Leninist
DDCs	District development committees

DDR	Disarmament, Demobilization and Reintegration
DRC	Dutch Reformed Church
ECOMOG	Economic Community of West African States Monitoring Group
ECOWAS	Economic Community of West African States
GDP	Gross domestic product
GSA	General services agency
HDR	Human development record
HOR	House of Representatives
ICG	International Crisis Group
ICRC	International committee of the Red Cross
ICTJ	International Centre for Transitional Justice
IDP	Internally displaced people
IEDS	Improvised explosive device
IFP	Inkatha Freedom Party
ILO	International Labour Organization
INGOs	International non-governmental organizations
INHRC	Independent national human rights commission
ITAC	International Technical Advisory Committee
JTMM	Jana Tantric Mukti Morcha
LURD	Liberia and the Liberians Unite for Reconciliation and Democracy
MoPR	Ministry of peace and reconciliation
MODEL	Movement for Democracy in Liberia
MJF	Madheshi Janadhikar Forum
MJFM	Madheshi Janadhikar Forum Madhesh
NC	Nepali Congress
NGOs	Non-governmental offices
NIS	National Intelligence Service
NP	National party

NPFL	National Patriotic Front of Liberia
NPRC	National People's Revolutionary Council
PAC	Pan Africanist Congress
PLA	People's liberation army
PRC	People's revolutionary council
RUF	Revolutionary United Front
SACP	South African Communist Party
SADF	South African Defence Force
SAP	South African Police
SLPP	Sierra Leone People's Party
SSC	State Security Council
TMLP	Tarai-Madhesh Loktantric Party
TRC	Truth and reconciliation commission
UCPN (Maoist)	Unified Communist Party of Nepal (Maoist)
UCPNM	Unified Communist Party of Nepal Maoists
UDF	United democratic Front
ULIMO	United Movement for Democracy
UML	Unified Marxist Leninist
UN	United Nations
UNDP	United Nations Development Programme
UNHCHR	United Nations High Commission for Human Rights
UNMIN	United Nations mission In Nepal
UN/OHCHR	United Nations/Office of the High Commissioner for Human Rights
UNOMSL	United Nations Observer Mission in Sierra Leone
USA	United States of America
VDCs	Village development committees

CHAPTER 1

Introduction

Introduction

The People's War (Maoist insurgency) in Nepal started in 1996 and ended in 2006 with the signing of the Comprehensive Peace Accord between the Maoist leader (Prachanda) and the Prime Minister of the Nepali Government (Girija Prasad Koirala). The People's War brought social chaos and disorder to Nepal. During this time, between 15000 and 16000 Nepalese were killed, 1350 were abducted and/or 'disappearanced'; nearly 6000 were left disabled and thousands of properties were stolen or destroyed. Theft, rape and abduction multiplied, infrastructure was destroyed and children were coerced into fighting for the insurgents (Dhruba, 2005; Gyawali, 2009; Hada, 2001; Himalayan Times, 2005; Nepal et al., 2011; Sapkota, 2004; Shakya, 2006; Thapa, 2004).

While the insurgency formally ended in 2006 with the Comprehensive Peace Accord (CPA), the peace process is still incomplete. In line with the CPA, a fundamental part of the peace process, a Constitutional Assembly (CA), was formed, Popular elections were held in 2008 and again, in 2013, but neither assembly could deliver an acceptable constitution for guiding the re-structuring of Nepalese society. However, each assembly was able to complete one significant part of the peace process. In 2012, 15,602 ex-Maoist insurgents voluntarily retired into Nepalese society with a smaller number, 1,444 being integrated into the re-organized Nepalese Army (Hamal, 2013; Shah, 2012; Subedi, 2012; Upreti, 2011). And in February 2015, nine years after the official end of the emergency (Kantipur, 2015), the Truth and Reconciliation Commission and The Commission on Enforced Disappearances were established. The aims of these commissions were to deliver justice to those who had experienced human rights violations during the insurgency and to create an atmosphere of reconciliation in Nepali society (Kantipur, 2015).

The focus of this book is an examination of the role of the Truth and Reconciliation Commission (TRC) in Nepal's peace process. Specifically, it will analyse and compare case studies on the role and successes of previous TRCs in South Africa, Liberia and Sierra Leone to examine the role the TRC might play in finalising Nepal's peace process.

Background

Before examining the peace process and the role of TRCs in implementing and facilitating peace processes, the causes and effects of the Maoist insurgency in Nepal must be explored as they have had a direct impact on the peace process in Nepal.

The armed struggle by the Maoists against the democratic government (it was still called His Majesty's Government even though the democracy was revived in 1990) began on February 13, 1996, when the Nepali Congress (NC) led coalition government failed to respond to the Maoists' 40-point demands concerning nationality, people's democracy and livelihood (Thapa, 2006, pp. 48, 53, 71). The Maoists demanded that a democratic, federal, secular state - free of discrimination and oppression - be established; that royal privileges be abolished; that the laws of the country be changed democratically; and that an extensive program of social and economic reforms in favour of the poor be enacted (Thapa, 2006, pp. 211-216). The ensuing insurgency disrupted the country and human rights violations were extreme.

According to the Ministry of Peace and Reconstruction, 89,571 people were internally displaced during the conflict and found refuge in the slums of the capital, Kathmandu (Hada, 2001; Sapkota, 2004). Abductions, disappearances, the targeted killing of civilians and the destruction of civilian property multiplied as the insurgency continued (IRIN, 2006). Approximately 1772 buildings belonging to Village Development Committees (VDCs) – the governmental local offices in the villages where social facilities like official recommendation letters and pensions were distributed to the local people by government representatives - were severely damaged; and 2,646 development structures were destroyed

(Dhruba, 2005; Gyawali, 2009; Nepal et al., 2011). The Nepalese education system deteriorated, as its services were disrupted or discontinued as a consequence of the insurgency (Shakya, 2009) and investment in Nepal's private sector steadily declined throughout the insurgency (Acharya, 2005; Upreti, 2010). Many investors, including joint ventures and multinational companies working in Nepal like Dabur Nepal, Surya Nepal, United Telecom Limited, Colgate Palmolive Nepal, Jyoti Spinning Mills, Unilever Nepal, and the Coca-Cola Company stopped production and sacked workers (Jha, 2011). External investors were unwilling to invest in Nepal and abandoned projects, for example, Norway withdrew from the Melamchi Drinking Water Project (Upreti, 2006).

10 years after the signing of the CPA, the hope and aspirations of the Nepalese people for peace and progress remain largely unfulfilled. The Nepalese people are frustrated with the delays that are primarily due to the conflicting interests of the major political parties; political mistrust, the absence of constitutional habits, the failure to enforce party laws and codes of conduct, and the formation of cross-coalitions of leaders to remain in power. The involvement of party leaders in corruption has further destabilised and delayed the peace process (Bhatta, 2012). The leaders of different parties like Jhalanath Khanal (Unified Marxist Leninist-UML), Sushil Koirala (Nepali Congress-NC), and Prachanda (Communist Party of Nepal-Maoist) have been publically rebuked by their own cadres because of their lack of responsiveness to Nepal's problems and in facilitating the peace process (Bhatta, 2013). Until these issues are resolved neither the peace process nor the human rights violations which occurred during the conflict will be effectively progressed or addressed.

Aim and objectives

This book explores the causes of the 10 year People's War in Nepal that disrupted the peace in peoples' lives. It also examines the continuing impacts on Nepal and assessed how a TRC could play an active and influential role in completing the country's peace process.

Following are the objectives of this book:

➢ Examine the background of the conflict in Nepal and identify key impacts of the conflict;

> ➤ Explores and analyses the role of the TRCs in other countries to assist in understanding the role of the TRC in Nepal so the Nepali TRC can facilitate and establish peace.

Rationale and Significance

Conflict refers to the struggle between two or more usually opposing parties pursuing divergent goals and limited resources to attain their respective goals. The struggle is normally aggressive and leads to violence. Such struggles break down interpersonal relationships between parties and commonly lead to destruction, loss of property and life. Thus, the restitution of relationships between disagreeing parties and addressing the causes of the conflict are two of the many challenges faced in post-conflict peace building.

There are a number of studies and reports on the conflict in Nepal. They include *Nepal country study on conflict transformation and peace building* (Eschborm, 2002); *The Maoist insurgency in Nepal, 1996-2008: Implications for U.S. counterinsurgency doctrine* (Kreuttner, 2001); *The Maoist insurgency of Nepal: Origin and evolution* (Muni, 2010); and *The Nepal conflict report* (United Nations High Commission for Human Rights [UNHCHR], 2012). According to these studies, and others, the consequences of the conflict in Nepal were overwhelmingly destructive (Baral, 2006; Hutt, 2004). But the insurgency also empowered the Nepalese people and ended monarchic rule. The empowerment of the people was not sufficient however to drive the peace process to completion so Nepal remains paralysed by the competing interests, indecision and inadequacies of the different political parties and this makes the country increasingly unstable. This book contributes further insights into the People's War in Nepal and the findings are of value to policy makers, administrators and scholars; policy makers may be guided to making more equitable policies, administrators may be assisted in implementing government programs and scholars may be further informed of the facts for educational purposes and future references.

Overview

This book is presented across 10 chapters. Chapter One establishes the research context, including a background to the Maoist insurgency and the beginning of the peace process in Nepal. The chapter also outlines the objectives and its significance.

Chapter Two presents the background of the conflict in Nepal, its causes and impacts. Chapter Three discusses the development of the peace process in Nepal, focusing on the ceasefires that occurred during the insurgency.

Chapter Four provides an overview of the characteristics and roles of Truth and Reconciliation Commissions in the peace process. It details the functions, powers and rules that guide a TRC.

Chapters Five, Six and Seven critically discuss the case studies of the TRCs from Liberia, Sierra Leone and South Africa respectively. Each chapter provides the background of the particular conflict/context and identifies its major consequences. Each analysis presents the objectives of the TRC, its findings and the recommendations made to address the problems. The strength and limitations (weaknesses) of each TRC are included in each chapter.

Chapter Eight analyses and compares the TRCs of the three countries. Specifically, the comparisons focus on the TRCs, their findings, and recommendations to facilitate the peace and reconciliation process in those countries.

Chapter Nine illustrates the TRC of Nepal with its objectives and situations. It details why the establishment of the Nepali TRC was delayed, why it is slow functioning and its progress to date.

Chapter 10 summarizes the discussion of the previous chapters and presents the major findings and objectives of this study that aim to provide suggestions to progress the functioning of the TRC of Nepal in establishing peace.

CHAPTER 2

Background of the Conflict

The nature of conflict varies relative to context and society. There are multidimensional ways of defining and analysing the nature of the conflict in Nepal, for instance, its political nature as evidenced by the clash between the current government regime and the armed opposition; as a social phenomenon where social structure is founded on a form of feudalism in the caste structure, as determined by the hegemony of tradition and religious beliefs; and as an economic phenomenon where specific groups of people dominate Nepalese society to the detriment of others in society (Baral, 2006, Hutt, 2004; Pathak, 2005).

Causes of the Conflict in Nepal

The present situation in Nepal is the result of a long and disastrous People's War (Katsiaficas, 2013). Pathak (2005) argues that the People's War initiated in Nepal in 1996 is an outcome of complex socioeconomic, legal and politico-ideological problems. The Maoists identified these problems and presented a list of demands that aimed to address the identified imbalances, specifically, the inequitable socioeconomic situations of the population, the confused political ideologies and the entrenched discrimination against the poorest Nepalis (Karki & Bhattarai, 2003). These problems reflected the different social, ethnic, economic and political dimensions of the country and sparked the insurgency (Hachchethu, 2005). The individual's consciousness played a vital role in understanding these complex problems (Thapa, 2004), as depicted by the energy and spread of the insurgency. Thus, the contributing factors can be divided into two categories namely socio-cultural and others such as individual and political factors.

Major: The socio-cultural factors

Nepal is a multi-dimensional country because of its multi-cultural, multi-ethnic, multi-religious and multi-lingual systems. Despite having 125 dialects and 61 ethnic groups (Bhattachan, 2001), the country's social, cultural, political, economic and educational structures are dominated and shaped by Hinduism, feudalism, and the Nepali language. The Hindu and "upper caste/class" people control most of the social and political sectors by occupying the highest ranks in the government sector thereby influencing and suppressing the minorities.

According to Deraniyagala (2005), economic aspects combined with social and political aspects played important roles in the growth and sustenance of the war in Nepal. Unemployment, insecurity, social discrimination and the dominant feudal structure of poor communities in Nepal contributed to the frustration of the people in remote areas and villages. Such discriminatory social practices, in place for 235 years since the unification of Nepal at the beginning of the Shaha dynasty and the late King Prithvi Narayan Shaha, were main causes behind the People's War (Upreti, 2004). The governing system of promoting and providing protection to the elite, as evidenced by the Land Reform Act in 1964 to establish tenancy rights also provided protection to the elite classes by the government and made the poor people poorer (Pathak, 2005). As a result, poverty is common in most of rural Nepal and this further contributed to the People's War.

According to Pandey (2005), the ethnic factor is an important element of the Maoist movement as changes in 1990 gave the Janajati ethnic group a new sense of identity and legal ground to appeal for their demands (Pandey, 2005 cited by Tiwari 2007). After a prolonged period of indifference, neglect and refusal, the oppressed ethnic groups began to demand their rights but their grievances were not heeded (Katsiaficas, 2013). The extreme economic disparities experienced by the majority of Nepalis motivated individuals to participate in the insurgency to overthrow the unequal socio-cultural system. Social and structural factors such as culture, religion, norms, rules and regulations also played a role or compelled people to engage in the armed insurgencies (Galtung, 1969; Galtung & Tschundi, 2001). The special attention the Maoists gave to the issues of non-discrimination and the rights to self-determination, particularly aimed at ethnic groups further fuelled the People's War (Maoists' 40 points demand, Demand No 20; Pathak, 2005; Yadav, 2016).

The structural perseverance of poverty, the continuing marginalization of ethnic minority groups and their increased inability to access state power and resources and the socio-economic inequality in Nepali society are widely recognised as catalysts for the People's War (Hutt, 2004; Joshi and Mason, 2007; Lawoti, 2005; Lawoti and Pahari, 2009). In the Nepali caste system, the indigenous and ethnic minorities were viewed as impure, inferior, dirty, ignorant, stupid and powerless; this stereotype contributed to and fuelled the structural violence. This is also why the Maoists strategically targeted the Dalits, the infamous "untouchables" that were most disadvantaged in caste- high illiteracy levels, landlessness and lack of political power (Mahat, 2005).

The untouchability of Dalits (so-called untouchable lower caste) still exists as a pervasive socio-cultural phenomenon in Nepal and there is a history of profound structural violence against them (Mahat, 2005). Dalits' life expectancy, literacy and income are far below the country's average (HDR, 2004). Dalits are discriminated against in employment and the government often fails to prosecute those who discriminate against them (DHRO, 2005). In an International Labour Organization (ILO) study on Nepal, approximately 48 percent of Dalits were denied employment due to their caste status and 21 percent had been refused jobs based on their caste status (ILO, 2005). In addition, approximately 71 percent of individuals were paid lower wages and salaries in both the private and informal sectors (ibid). Due to this marginalization and dis-empowerment in political and civil services, the Dalits and other minority groups were ready to support the People's War.

The Maoists understood this oppression and channelled it into the insurgency as an expression of ethnic power. The ethnic groups were easily integrated into the Maoist insurgency both as an expression of their collective identity and as a way of breaking their subservience to the long historic mistreatment experienced under the socio-cultural hegemony of the high caste land-owning Hindu elite (Shakya, 2006). The Maoists considered the root causes of the social problems in Nepal to be the constitution and the palace so they targeted them to help unify the rest of the country. In this way, they were able to attract many frustrated people, mainly from rural areas, and this helped the growth of the ongoing rebellion.

Rogers (1960) posits that changes that have the potential to alter the practises of a society are often caused by outsiders; these outsiders, on their own or as representatives of a program of planned change, introduce new ideas to achieve definite goals. In Nepal, the Maoists represent the outsiders due to their political ethics that brought both new ideas (rejecting democratic politics for violence) and definite goals (social justice) that captured the imagination of the people, especially of the peasants, ethnic groups of people, Dalits and the youth of their respective societies.

The minority groups felt there was no other choice for them to show their existence after the ruling government's refusal to heed their demands. Pyakurel (2001), quoting William Zartman's conclusion, emphasises this point "if a group, community or a party feels that its existence and identity are in crisis, it is forced to make tough choices" (p.112-113). Thus, the persistent oppression drove the indigenous and Dalits to choose insurgency to escape their threatened existence.

The Maoist insurgency (People's War) was thus driven by the convergence of socio-cultural factors present in Nepali society (Venhaus, 2010), ethnic exclusion, as discussed above, and gender inequality (Gautam, Baskota & Manchanda, 2001; Gurung, 2005; Gautam, Leve, 2007; Parvati, 2003).

Nepal is a patriarchal society. In the Hindu patriarchal value system, man is placed at a higher stratum, while a woman is given a very low status in the society. Moreover, women from the indigenous and Dalit groups are more discriminated against, constantly being reminded and made to realize that they are from the inferior group and being subjected to gender-based violence such as sexual abuse and child marriage, limited access to and control over resources, unpaid and low wage few job opportunities (Shakya, 2006).

Although Nepal ratified the Convention on the Elimination of All Forms of Discrimination against Women (CEDAW) in 1991 without reservation (BBC, 2014; Government of Nepal, 2011), Nepali society discriminates against women in the areas of social, economic, political and family life, including citizenship, inheritance, marriage, adoption, and domestic and foreign employment (GoN, 2011). Gender discrimination against women is very high in Nepal and this was a major contributing factor for so many women participating as combatants in the Maoist insurgency (People's War). According to the United Nations, of the 19,602 people making up the People's Liberation Army (PLA), 3,846 were women (United Nations (2007) cited by Arino, 2008).

Although all the national political parties had given priority to gender issues they had failed to implement practically. For instance, there was not a single woman included in Constitution Recommendation Committee and National Planning Commission until the insurgency. So, the demands for gender equality, justice and non-discrimination made by the Maoists attracted the rural women (Pathak, 2005). Among the Maoist's 40 point demands, one was to stop the patriarchal exploitation and discrimination against women, for example, by allowing daughters to inherit parental property. However, this could only be achieved if gender equality was advocated in this area. The Maoists widely explained this ideology to Nepali women through political gatherings, cultural programs, the party media and mass print media. Many women were influenced and interested to achieve their rights and became active participants in the Maoist insurgency (People's War) as combatants. As Thapa (2005) explains:

> Another notable characteristic of the Maoist insurgency is the degree of women's participation in guerrilla ranks. Women's political participation in the past had been limited to electoral areas, especially in voting and occasional candidacy in elections. It is a big surprise that Nepali women now have joined a guerrilla organization under arms (p.11).

The individual factors which led women to join the war included women's liberation, equality of opportunity within Maoist organizations and the Maoists' social reform programs. These included campaigns against alcohol, gambling, sexual violence and exploitation. According to International Centre for Transitional Justice (ICTJ), for example, (2010):

> In areas where Maoists exercised effective control, they prohibited domestic violence, child marriage or abuse, prostitution, extra-marital affairs, alcoholism and gambling. They started to enforce these policies through "people's courts", imposing punishments including imprisonment, which was sometimes accompanied by labor and fines (p. 11).

The issues raised by the Maoists, thus, attracted women to fight for equal access to inheritance rights, the elimination of patriarchal exploitation and discrimination, equal payment for equal work, and an end to the sexual exploitation of low caste women. Other factors that motivated many women to join the insurgency included poverty, unemployment, low success in national level school exam and the low social status and condition of widows (Pyakurel, 2006).

The emancipation of bonded laborers was another social cause that fuelled the People's War in Nepal, particularly the emancipation of at least 16,000 bonded laborers (Kamaiya) in western Nepal by the Nepali government on 17 July 2000 (Fujikura, 2007, p.329). As the state was unable to settle their issues after declaring their emancipation as they were left without houses or land, they began to confiscate land from the landlords, according to the instructions of the Maoist party (Shahu, 2013).

Adams and Bradsbury (1995) assert that culture and religion have been the greatest causes for the protracted conflict in Nepal. Although many religions like Buddhism, Bon and Kirat are practiced in Nepal, Hinduism was the official state religion until the Interim Constitution of Nepal 2007. There was a tendency to subsume other religions into Hinduism however which meant people were not free to practice their own religions (Shakya, 2006). The suppression of people's culture and religion of the majority by the upper class minority thus exacerbated and protracted the conflict (Shakya, 2006).

The People's War was largely based on class and caste/ethnicity (Bhattachan, 2000). As Sharma (2002) states, Nepali upper classes had a long time practised oppression, discrimination and exploitation against other nationalities, religions and tribes. The consolidation of elites in the management of the country, as well as in the civil services, exacerbated this discrimination. Since the mid 1980's, the number of civil service employees from the most economically and politically powerful ethnicities in Nepal has risen from 69% to 98% (Thapa & Sijapati, 2003). The lack of political representation in the government was also one of the causes in the participation of lower caste (Dalit), ethnic people in the Maoist insurgency (People's War). In general election of 1999, not a single member of the House of Representatives was a Dalit (Bhattachan et al, 2009). Dalits are also significantly under-represented in the civil service and judicial system. As Baniya (2007) indicates,

As 1854 survey revealed that 98 percent of all civil services posts were held by "upper-caste" *Brahmins* and *Chetris*. Over a century later, 1991 survey indicates that 93 percent of these posts are still held by upper-caste *Brahmins* and *Chetris*. Within a 137-year period, there was only a five percent increase in Nepal's political diversity (p.49).

According to a 2001 census, while Brahmins constitute only 16 percent of the population, they represent 57 percent of parliament and 89 percent of the judiciary (Dalit NGO Federation Nepal, 2001). This pattern of exclusion is repeated at the local government level, where Dalits and other minority groups are severely underrepresented in the administrative system (HRW, 2010). Of the more than 3,000 Village Development Committees chairmen, only a handful are Dalits (Baniya, 2007; ILO, 2005) and this discrimination also persists in the (then) Royal Nepal Army (Baniya, 2007).

Accordingly, the inequality the majority of the population experienced undoubtedly contributed to their willingness to accept the call for radical, violent action that would dramatically disrupt the social, political and economic order. As Thapa and Sijapati (2003) observe, this "hope in a radical solution," was a function of poverty rather than a consequence of Maoist ideology and the Maoist insurgency (People's War) can be considered as a "rage against a long legacy of oppression based on caste and ethnicity" (Sengupta, 2005 cited by Do & Iyer, 2007, p.3).

Other Factors

Other factors can be divided into political and individual which are described below.

Political Factors

Political ideologies were another cause of the People's War in Nepal and they became a key factor for participating in the insurgency (Hudson, 1999; Bandura, 2003). The varied elements of politics within a country influence the ideologies of people; political strategies as well as governance play a role in the development of an insurgency. In Nepal, parliamentary politics and the politicians were corrupt. The competition to grab power and position in the government by the competing political parties made the political situation increasingly unstable (Hachhethu, 2005, p. 11). Nepal's many minority populations were effectively excluded from parliament as they had no political representation, few expectations and little autonomy (Gersony, 2003; Gurung, 2005; Hossain, Siitonen & Sharma, 2006; Hutt, 2004; Leve, 2007; Parvati, 2003; Pettigrew & Shneiderman, 2004; Thapa, 2004). Because the indigenous and marginalized groups had minimal or no political representation, their grievances increased yet participation in policy making, as well as decision-making processes, were not considered because of their suppression by the government (Do & Iyer, 2007). The worsening political situation caused by poor governance strategies and the personal pre-occupations of politicians resulted in bad governance and inequitably distributed development (Hossain et al, 2006; Kumar, 2003; Leve, 2007; Pathak, 2005) which frustrated the people, actively pushing them into rebellion.

The regressive characteristics and criminalization rife in Nepali politics made the ground fertile for the People's War. As the NC was in power, its cadres were more irresponsible and severe against their opponents, like the UPF, forgetting the reality that all have equal rights in democracy. Passing the IMT with a sharp contradiction, dispatching parliamentary members to minimize the vote against themselves (the NC Prime Minister Ser Bahadur Deuwa), voting against their own government during the no-confidence motion in 1997 are examples which made the general people rally against the incumbent political leaders and institutions (Pathak, 2005). Thus the government's failure to address these issues and represent the problems of Nepali society the People's War and provided the circumstances for the Maoists to mobilize the marginalized and oppressed populations to join or support the insurgency (Joshi & Mason, 2007).

Hachhethu (2005) observes that:

The post-1990 politics were characterized by anarchy as depicted by several events. The parliamentary elections were called off four times; recommendations for dissolution of the House of Representatives (HOR) were made six times; special sessions of the HOR were attended seven times; and the government changed thirteen times due to power games. The Maoists have constantly gained the strength exploiting the weakness of its opponent, the state (p.11).

Despite the transition to democracy in 1990, traditional elites and upper castes continued to dominate the state apparatus and left wing parties were marginalized within the political process (Deraniyagala, 2005, p.56). Pervasive control of local and national leadership posts by "upper-caste" members of the same feudal figures resulted in wholesale disregard for Dalit issues, while attempts at building effective Dalit political movements were met with punitive violence (JUP, 2001). This resulted in political instability and conflict because the political parties could not make clear and far-sighted visions, programs and decisions about the development of the country. Sedan and Hussein (2002) mention that;

> [After] a short period of considerable optimism, it became increasingly evident that the new political order was characterized by instability, corruption and patronage (a crisis of governance) and that a rapid succession of governments was unable to achieve any real headway in addressing Nepal's continuing economic underdevelopment and deep-seated social inequalities. In this already unstable context – and ostensibly in response to it – an armed insurgency began in February 1996, led by Nepali Maoists (p.9).

The extremely poor performance of the government, the lack of institutionalized bureaucracy, and the frequent changes and lack of direction created an environment where people were not represented by a real democracy and did not feel safety. History also shows many hidden and neglected aspects that fostered the People's War in Nepal. Seddon and Hussein (2002) clearly and strongly argue that:

> A historical perspective reveals that a failure of development and of governance created the pre-conditions – poverty, inequality, social discrimination and lack of social justice and democracy – for widespread discontent, and ultimately for the Maoist insurgency. Not only has the government been ineffective in providing for the needs of the poor, it is generally seen and experienced as corrupt, repressive and as working against, not for, the interests of ordinary people. International and national development agencies have also failed to strengthen the capacity and commitment of state structures or to change practices at local level to any marked degree (p.8).

The misuse of international donations through International Non Governmental Organizations (INGOs)/Non Governmental Organizations (NGOs) also frustrated the poor, disadvantaged, marginalized and vulnerable people as the elites or feudal people benefited. The Rapti Rural Area Development Project (RADP) by USAID that was in place (USAID/Nepal, 2000) for 15 years only reached the elites due to bad politics (Pathak, 2005).

The outcome of such events was to enable the Maoists to source many Nepalis as the manpower to instigate their insurgency while the Nepalis found in the Maoists, a platform from which to fight against the government for their basic rights.

The people's uprising during the 1990s developed from the push for the rights of ethnic identity and civic consciousness. During this period, the dominance of the so-called upper class (Brahmin and Chhetri) was questioned (Bista, 1991).

Individual Factors

Different causes such as social injustice, oppression, greed, exploitation, and economic necessity contribute to an individual performing different, drastic actions such as looting and/or joining a rebel group to kill other people to take revenge. The lack of fulfilment of needs may drive an individual to join an armed insurgency because the individual feels that the insurgency is the only way to achieve fulfilment and end their problems (Mitchell, 1981; Venhaus, 2010). Collier and Sambanis (2002) and Weinstein (2002) further support this notion and use economic endowment, or materialistic gain theory, to explain possible motivations for individuals to join a rebellion.

In Nepal, 31% of people live below the poverty line, as indicated by the Human Development Record (HDR-2015). Poverty diminishes people's capacity to satisfy their own needs as well as those of their families. It may lead them to engage in any activity which promises high returns for gratification of needs, such as insurgency. Many individual Nepalis lived with the reality of shattered dignity, ideology, religion and economic inequality in a society dominated by a high caste, privileged social elite and a royalist state that oppressed them. Poverty was one of the contributing factors to the Maoist insurgency (People's War) (Devarajan, 2005; Leve,

2007; Macours, 2010; Parwez, 2006), with most of the Maoist insurgents being young men from the poorest rural districts of Nepal (Sharma, 2006). They joined the insurgency with a view to end fundamental social and economic problems.

The Maoists thus identified and used the social problems of inequality, exclusion and discrimination based on gender, caste, class, and ethnicity to accelerate their insurgency (Marks, 2007; Sharma, 2004). According to Marks and Sharma,

> The goals of the CPN (M) were to establish a Maoist people's republic, end Indian imperialism in Nepal, eliminate the caste system, and stop ethnic, religious, and linguistic exploitation. Following Maoist doctrine, the CPN (M) established support in the remote, impoverished areas where poor infrastructure limited government reach (pp. 303-304; 42-49).

The activities and behaviour of the Nepali police and army towards the people also played a major role in continuing the insurgency. Police violence and repression turned many people into insurgents to protect themselves from such abuse, as well as to take revenge (Hossain, Siitonen and Sharma, 2006; Singh, Dahal and Mills, 2005). The rape and sexual abuse of girls and women by the police during their operations to suppress the insurgency led to people supporting the insurgency for revenge and to prevent further violations. Pathak (2005) reports that human rights violations by the army drove men to flee from their homes to hide in the safety of the jungle. The police then described these men as wanted fugitives (pp; 123, 137); such abuses of power by the legal authorities, the violations and criminal behaviours of those in positions of authority caused many ordinary Nepali men and women to join the insurgency.

Consequences of the Conflict in Nepal

Any form of violence or social conflict leaves behind physical scars, not only on the people, but also on the whole country evidences by damaged buildings; the displacement of individuals and families; disrupted public services (Pathak, 2005). The Maoists' 'People's War' brought different painful effects to Nepal. During the conflict, the nation's most important economic sectors, tourism and agriculture, were severely disrupted. Although it is 10 years after the CPA, the lack of development of Nepal's political economy reflects an uneasy social peace that can be attributed to a peace process which is effectively paralyzed by a number of factors, as discussed below.

Socio-cultural consequences

The Maoist insurgency (People's War) affected the lives of 23 million people directly in Nepal (Himalayan News Service, 2003). The continued violence resulted in the breakdown of social and communal bonds as the kinship networks and neighborhood relationships that bound communities disintegrated because of fear, distrust and loss of self-confidence (DTIC, 2005).

The decade-long Maoist insurgency (People's War) destabilized Nepal's socio-cultural structures causing widespread terror and insecurity. This affected people's basic rights and livelihoods and increased the population of widows, orphans and internal refugees. The police, the army, and the Maoists were responsible for thousands of deaths (murders), as well as numerous abuses of human rights during the conflict (Human Rights Watch, 2008). Jha (2011) indicates that,

"As many as 16,000 people were killed by the rebel Maoists and the security forces... 5,800 people were left disabled, 89,571 people were internally displaced, 25,000 children were orphaned, 9,000 women were widowed and 1350 people disappeared" (p.14).

The death toll included children, teachers, students, social workers, civilians, politicians, farmers, lawyers, health workers, laborers, businessmen, army, police, armed police, civil servants and 341 children less than 17 years of age (INSEC, 2005).

The social and traditional ways of life of the people were deeply disrupted, or, in many cases, ruined. The indigenous Nepalis and Dalits were mistreated, abused and trapped by both the government forces and the Maoists during the insurgency. The Maoists forced Dalits to make homemade guns (Khukuri) and sew combat wear. The State tortured them for aiding the Maoists and barred them from their professions as tailors, cobblers, blacksmiths (Shakya, 2006). According to DTIC (2005),

Maoists interfered in cultural affairs, for example, by banning the performance of the last tribute ritual function (Kriya) by the people.

They have brutally arrested people *(Kriya Putri)* individuals taking part in the rites. They stopped other traditional celebrations in the countryside as well. Maoists also did not allow teaching *Sanskrit* as the Brahmin language. Such activities carried out by the Maoist have caused widespread social disruption (I-49).

The frequent strikes, security checks, blockades, shutdowns, beatings, threats, humiliation, forced prostitution, social isolation, rape and sexual harassment, made life in Nepal hard, hazardous and unpredictable during the insurgency. Women, especially those who were young and unmarried, were the most vulnerable in the rural areas. Many fled from their villages to avoid the atrocities committed by the opposing forces (Upreti, 2010, p. 260). As Upreti (2010) indicated:

> In order to avoid atrocities in the villages, over 70,000 of the girls aged between 15 and 30 years were compelled to leave their homes and join restaurants as dancers and waitresses. The situation turned to be so precarious that many of them had no choice but to enter into immoral practices like prostitution in major townships of the country (p. 260).

The insurgency forced almost 300,000 people to leave their native places (Annapurna Post, 2005; Caritas Nepal, 2005). About 90,000 people who lived in slums of Kathmandu were internally displaced (Hada, 2001) and about 2 million people out of the total population 25 to 29 million Nepalis (NBS, 2005) fled to overseas countries mostly to Gulf countries and India for employment and to save their lives (irinnews.org). The Relief and Rehabilitation Division of Peace and Reconstruction Ministry in 2011 recorded that 89,171 internally displaced people (IDP) applied for relief packages from the government (GoN, 2011).

Shakya (2006) also describes that:

> During the conflict many people were displaced. Some of the groups who were displaced were VDC secretaries, teachers, political cadres, and youths. People left their homes and communities for their security. The first targets of Maoist were the feudal landlords. Many of them were either killed, tortured or displaced. However, their displacement, on the contrary had negative impacts on poor

people as the local people could not get jobs. Those who were not ready to give forced donations, too had to flee (p. 7).

According to Gyawali (2009), the armed conflict severely affected the educational system, especially in some rural areas. In Rolpa and Rukum where the Maoist party had grown, the schools were targeted and school pupils were used as human shields, porters, housekeepers, cooks, sex slaves or/and abducted for ransom (Gyawali, 2009). Nearly 3,000 teachers stopped teaching and 700 schools were closed (ibid). Maoists killed 60 teachers and 66 students for not providing physical and economical help, caused the 'disappearance' of 151 teachers and abducted 516 students and 62 teachers. The Nepali state forces killed 44 teachers, 172 students, detained 158 teachers and 115 students; and had 14 teachers 'disappear' (Himalayan Times, 2005; Gyawali, 2009). This affected the education of children in major ways both in terms of access and reintegration in education (Shakya, 2006).

Physical Consequences

The infrastructure of the nation was severely damaged during the insurgency. Maoists destroyed drinking water systems, telecommunication towers, barracks, suspension bridges, and hydro power plants, the electrical grid, transmission lines and power substations, historical monuments, government offices including Village Development Committee Offices and adjacent health posts (clinics), police posts and agricultural training centres. In this way, rural people were deprived of many basic social needs (Shakya, 2009; Gyawali, 2009).

According to the Ministry of Local Development (2002) and National Planning Commission (2003), an estimated 177 private houses, 33 heath centres, 12 telecommunication towers, 31 school buildings, 100 police posts, 18 post offices, 93 government offices, 29 private offices, 1300 Village Development Committee (VDC) buildings and 31 electricity related centres were destroyed. Similarly, there was damage to Jhimruk hydroelectricity installations (12MW), Adhikhola hydroelectricity (5MW) and Modi hydroelectricity (14MW) during 2003. About 14 domestic airports in remote areas also suffered substantial damage (ibid) as did 112 telephone stations and substations in 45 out of 75 districts in Nepal (Nepal Telecom, 2004); 26 bridges, public buses (no statistics available), private vehicles (no statistics available) were also attacked and destroyed during the Maoist insurgency (People's War) (Department of Road, 2005).

The rebel forces targeted banks; particularly the state-owned banks as well as the micro financial institutions and even the local Small Farmer Co-operatives were not spared (Hofmann & Grossmann, 2005). The destruction and looting of bank buildings after May 2002 was estimated at US$ 11.5 million in cash, jewellery and gold (ECON, 2002). As banks were being looted and robbed, any situated in remote and rural areas were withdrawn which directly impacted the economic development of the nation.

A problem created by the armed conflict (People's War) was landmines and Improvised Explosive Devices (IEDs) in rural areas which were used by government and Maoist forces during the Maoist insurgency (Upreti, 2006). Children and women are the most vulnerable to these hidden devices. In 2006, 98 adults and children, and in 2007, 169 adults and children were injured by these weapons (Shakya, 2009). Until these weapons are located and destroyed, the peace and peace process will not be completed.

Political Economy Consequences

The armed conflict caused devastating economic consequences in Nepal. Agriculture, industry, employment, and foreign aid - the major economic sectors – were severely disrupted or discontinued (Pradhan, n.d.; Jha, 2010). Nepal's gross domestic product (GDP) dropped to 0.8 percent in 2001/2002, was 4.8 percent in 2001 and 2.6 percent in 2005. Private sector investment in agriculture, carpet, garment, textile, tobacco, beverage, declined from 15.4 percent to 12.6 percent between 1996 and 2004 (Acharya, 2005; Upreti, 2010; Jha, 2010). As Nepal is an agriculture-based country, two-thirds of the labor force are engaged in this sector and contributed one-third of Nepal's GDP (Karkee, 2008). The budget in the agricultural sector dropped to 1% of the GDP between 2001 and 2004 when the insurgency was at its peak (Jha, 2010). According to the Ministry of Finance (2008), this sector's growth rate had been 2.7 percent per annum in the 1990s and 2.8 percent from 2001 to 2006. In 1991, agriculture's share in GDP was 45 percent, 37 percent in 2001 and 33 percent in 2007 (ibid).

The development activities declined significantly during the conflict period. Between 2001/02 and 2004/05, the development expenditure of the government declined from Rs.50.47 billion to Rs.47.20 billion (National Planning Commission, 2005). In most of the Village Development

Committees (VDCs) and District Development Committees (DDCs), development activities were halted as the resources for the development were diverted to other sectors, mainly to the army and police. Many of the farmers in different parts of the country left agricultural land uncultivated and investment in the agricultural sector declined to as low as 1 percent (Jha, 2010)

The lack of economic opportunities within Nepal caused the younger generations to migrate overseas. The recent trend shows a steady flow of Nepalis to Asian, European, American and Golf countries, and many more, for skilled and unskilled jobs (Gautam, 2008: Journal of sociology). This was accelerated by unemployment as well as high under-unemployment and later conflict (1996 – 2006) in Nepal (Sharma Paudel, n.d.). Unstable government, repeated strikes and closure and investment unfriendly environment in Nepal cause further loss of confidence in Nepali youth.

Tourism is the backbone of Nepal's economy and it has been affected heavily by the insurgency. The reduction of foreign investment in tourism industries has seriously threatened Nepal's economy (Gyawali, 2011; Upreti, 2006) with the political turmoil triggered by the violent revolution seeing the number of visitors in 2002 (275,468) falling to the level of 1990 (254,885) (Bhattarai, Conway, & Shrestha, 2004; GoN, 2015). Moreover, because tourism is strongly linked with other Nepali industries, the downturn in the tourism negatively impacted up to 80 percent of other industries in the country (Pradhan, n.d.). In terms of lost output, between 1996 and 2006, Nepal lost US$315 million (Pradhan, n.d.). According to IDA,

> Roughly 3.9 million tourists arrived in Nepal by air in 1996 bringing with them foreign exchange worth 119 million in US dollars. Since then the tourist inflow in Nepal has declined steadily from one year to next. Since the 1996/97 tourist seasons, tourist arrivals have decreased by one-half, largely due to the insurgency. The flow of foreign exchange into Nepal has likewise decreased (I-46).

The political arena in Nepal after the Maoist Insurgency (People's War) has also significantly changed as successive post-2006 governments have failed to win people's confidence. As Bhatta (2013) explains, the underlying causes of 10 years of Maoist insurgency (People's War) remain unresolved and partly because time has generated more losers than winners. There might be many reasons behind this and one of them is that the new social contract constructed after 2006 political change could not embrace a common national identity. The old political class, for their part, has been abolished and the new political class has not been able to win people's confidence.

Since the insurgency some positive changes have occurred; the oppressed ethnic, indigenous, Dalits and women have gained some position in the society. Nepal functioned under the caste system for centuries but the insurgency helped lower caste people rise up to claim their social rights. As a result, the domination of upper caste over lower castes has been minimized and special quotas have been provided in every sector by the Government, as well as in the private sectors, to enhance their level of life (Gyawali, 2009).

There has been a radical increase in the representation of the women in the Constitution Assembly. This has risen from around 7 percent, 18 out of 265, in the 1999 elections to 32.27 percent, 197 out of 601, in the CA elections in 2008 and 30 percent, 172 out of 575, in the CA elections in 2013 (NEC, 1999, 2008, 2013).

Nepal, as a patriarchal society allowed men to marry another woman if the first one died or did not give birth to children. In contrast, widows had to wear a white dress without any ornaments for the rest of her life, irrespective of her age. Since the uprising, traditional assumptions have shifted; widows can now wear colourful dresses and ornaments and remarry (Gyawali, 2009). The traditional assumptions that girls and women should be coy, docile, shy and fearful have faded away; their self-confidence and self-expression conveys that the 'culture of silence' has been broken to a large extent. As Shakya (2009) observes, Nepali women have succeeded in breaching the traditional patriarchal value system. The People's War has thus contributed to eroding the hackneyed stereotype of women as passive and defenceless victims of armed violence (Arino, 2008).

CHAPTER 3

Background of the Peace Process

The Ceasefire: The beginning of the Peace Process

The People's War was concluded in different steps through peace talks and the signing of the peace agreement. However, while the insurgency has ended and significant changes have occurred in Nepalese society through the dynamic of the peace process, peace has not yet been established.

The restoration of peace required the resolution of conflict. The Government and Maoists had met, discussed and declared a ceasefire twice before beginning a negotiated peace process in 2005; in 2001 and 2003 during the insurgency period (Pathak, 2005; BBC, 2006). The peace talks were facilitated and supported by internal as well as external powers including international government, non-governmental organisations (Mishra, 2004; Kelly, 2009; Lawoti and Pahari, 2009; Thapa, 2004; Ghimire, 2006; Vaughn cited in Kreuttner, 2013) India (Mishra, 2004; Dhungana, 2006) the United States of America (Meheta, 2004) and China (Hutt, 2004; Vaughn, 2006) were the external powers as the mediators involved in the peace talks between two warring parties, the Government and the Maoists (Communist Party of Nepal-Maoist). When the insurgency began, the United States, the United Kingdom and India supported the Nepalese government by providing helicopters, training and moral support to the Royal Nepal Army. (Kreuttner, 2013) These countries reduced their support and acted as the peace mediators after the King's coup in 2005 (Upreti, 2010; Kreuttner, 2013) claiming they opposed the King's anti-democratic action (Vaughn cited in Kreuttner, 2013). The Maoist and the main stream political parties then joined forces to oppose the King; this helped to bring about the peace talks, the signing of the peace agreement and the abolitions of the Constitutional Monarchy (Surhke, 2009).

The peace talks occurred in different stages which ultimately brought the ceasefire and end of the insurgency in Nepal.

Stage I

As the Chairman of the Maoist Party, Pushpa Kamal Dahal (Prachanda) stated on the 6th anniversary of the People's War in February 2002, "We are ready to be involved in talks, dialogue, fronts or show some flexibility ... We have never closed the door for talks to find a political solution, and we will never do so in the future" (Thapa cited in Surhke, 2009, p.5). The Government and the Maoists declared a joint ceasefire on 23 July 2001 to discuss the establishment of peace. At the same time, Mr. Deuba, a senior leader of the Nepali Congress (NC) party, became the Prime Minister. Deuba, supported the talks and the Maoists welcomed him positively. Upreti (2006) argues that the Maoists declared a ceasefire when the new government led by Deuba was formed. They believed that they could use the ceasefire to negotiate their grievances with the new government. The government and the Maoists held three meetings on 30 August, 11 September and 13 November, in 2001 (ibid).

Table: 3.1 First Ceasefire Meeting

	State	Maoist
Dialogue Team	Mr. Chiranjibi Wagle-Coordinator	Mr. Krishna Bahadur Mahara- Coordinator
	Mr. Mahesh Acharya	Mr. Top Bahadur Magar
	Mr. Bijaya Gacchedar	Mr. Agni Prasad Sapkota
	Mr. Narahari Acharya	
First Meeting	30 August 2001, Place: Godavari	
Second Meeting	11 September 2001, Place: Bardia	
Third Meeting	13 November 2001, Place: Gidavari	
Facilitators	Mr. Daman Nath Dhungana	
	Mr. Padma Ratna Tuladhar	
Break down	By attacking on Army Barrack by Maoists	

(Source: IDA, 2005)

The first meeting on the 30 August discussed the creation of a new constitution and the end of Constitutional Monarchy. The Maoists were ready to compromise on the question of the monarchy because of its popularity with the Nepalese people. The meeting concluded without any decisions made. At the second meeting on 11 September nothing was resolved except that a third meeting would be convened. In the third meeting on 13 November, the Maoist members were again ready to compromise on the issue of monarchy but they demanded that an interim government be established and elections for a Constituent Assembly be held to draft a new constitution (Dahal, 2006, p. 9). The government wanted royal power to remain dominant but the Maoists rejected such an outcome. The Maoist talked about a multiparty parliamentary democracy which was non-negotiable for the existing government. These first-stage negotiations failed because the parties could not reach a compromise on the future governance of Nepal (Shimkhada et al, 2005).

Stage II

Sagar Chettri representing the Maoists and Minister Narayan Singh Pun on behalf of Government signed a ceasefire agreement on 29 January, 2003 (Thapa, 2005) that initiated the second stage for the establishment of peace in Nepal. In this stage; four dialogues were held in April, May (twice) and August 2003. During these talks, the United Nations (UN) and some (I) NGOs- International Committee of the Red Cross (ICRC), Amnesty Nepal, Centre for Humanitarian Dialogue, Carter Centre, The European Union (EU) worked as facilitators and mediators to help in establishing the peace (Upreti, 2006).The UN official, Tamrat Samuel, an American was central to these negotiations (Whitfield, 2008) to communicate the conditions of the ceasefire and peace process between the Maoists and the Government.

Table: 3.2 Second Ceasefire Meeting

	State	Maoist
Dialogue Team	Mr. Narayan Singh Pun	Dr. Baburam Bhattarai
	Dr. Upendra Devkota	Mr. Krishna Bahadur Mahara
	Mr. Badri Prasad Mandal	
	Mrs. Anuradha Koirala	Mr. Ram Bahadur Badal
	Mr. Ramesh Nath Pandey	
	Dr. Prakash Chandra Lohani	
	Mr. Kamal Thapa	

	State	Maoist
First Meeting	27 April 2003, Place: Kathmandu	
Second Meeting	9 May 2003, Place: Kathmandu	
Third Meeting	24 May 2003, Place: Dang	
Fourth Meeting	17-19 August 2003, Place: Dang	
Facilitators	Mr. Karnadhoj Adhikari	
	Mr. Padma Ratna Tuladhar	
	Mr. Daman Nath Dhungana	
	Mr. Sailendra Upadhyaya	
Break down	By killing high ranking Army official by Maoists	

(Source: IDA, 2005)

During the ceasefire, both warring parties broke the codes of conduct. The state killed 80 people and the Maoists killed 47 people (IDA, 2005). As a result, the Maoists ended the ceasefire in August 2003, stating that the Government failed to consider their demand of a new Constitutional Assembly. "The process was additionally complicated..., the position of the Maoists on their fundamental political issue of the Constituent Assembly had already become a make-or-break issue, comparable to the end of negotiations in November 2001" (Thapa, 2005, p.8).

On the failure of the second stage peace talks, the political, social and economical situation worsened as resources were utilized to strengthen the military capacities of the opposing combatants (Simkhada et al, 2005)

> The Government utilized the ceasefire period to strengthen its military capabilities in terms of arms, intelligence, training and the physical identification of the Maoist leaders and cadres. In turn, Maoists utilized the opportunity to gain the release of their cadres from jail, force withdrawal of cases filed by the government against them on the court of law, expand public contact, promote their political agenda and recruit, train and mobilize additional militia (p.61).

Stage III

The third stage of the peace talks took place in 2005 when the Maoist called for a three month ceasefire from 3 September to 2 December. During the year, the King had seized all the powers of the state and the Maoist and parliamentary political parties united against the monarchy demanding a reconstruction of the country's political order. As Surhke (2009) determined:

> On 1 February 2005, the King dissolved the parliament, imprisoned politicians, cracked down on the media, and declared an emergency... the Maoists and the mainstream political parties – now in opposition to the King ... Both stood to gain from a restructuring of the state. (p. 6)

A 12 point understanding, mediated by India, was finally agreed upon and signed by the Maoists along with seven participating political parties and the Nepali government on 22 November 2005 in New Delhi, India (Thapa, 2005). It was supported by International/National Non-Government Organisations ((I) NGOs) such as UN, International Committee of the Red Cross (ICRC), Amnesty International, Centre for Humanitarian Dialogue and Carter Centre, as well as Amnesty Nepal (Upreti, 2006). As this agreement says "it has become the need of the hour to establish peace by resolving the armed conflict being for the past 10 years through progressive political outlet ...the understanding has been reached..." (12 point understanding, 2005, p.1).

The 12 points understanding included:

1. The democracy, peace, prosperity, social advancement and independent, sovereign Nepal is the principal wish of all the Nepali people.

2. The agitating parties are fully committed to the fact that the existing conflict in the country can be resolved and that the sovereignty and the state powers can be vested completely in people only by establishing full democracy by restoring the parliament.

3. Firmly committed to establishing permanent peace by bringing the existing armed conflict in the country to an end through a progressive political outlet of the establishment of the full democracy by ending the autocratic monarchy and holding the constituent assembly election.

4. Commitment in institutionalization of governance, human rights and rule of law.

5. Commitment to create an environment to allow to return the displaced people.

6. Self-assessment and self-criticism of the past mistakes and weaknesses.

7. Not repeat such mistakes and weaknesses.

8. Respect the human rights and press freedom.

9. Election of municipality.

10. Commitment to protect the independence, sovereignty, geographical integrity and national unity of the country.

11. Invite all Nepali people to make the movement successful.

12. Investigate the inappropriate conduct that took place in the past by political parties.

The agreement clarified the issue of constituent assembly election, formation of a multiparty parliamentary system and the creation of a democratic constitutional monarchy. Wakugawa at el (2011) explained that "The parties had arrived at general principles of restructuring, issued in the form of a 12-point understanding that embraced constituent assembly elections, multiparty democracy and an end to autocratic monarchy". The 12-point understanding created the path for a final peace agreement: the Comprehensive Peace Accord (CPA) which provided a roadmap for further developments in the peace process. The 12 point understanding also fixed conditions between the insurgent parties and eased misunderstanding during the peace process (Capoccia &Daniel, 2007).

The CPA that was signed on 21 November 2006 to end the People's War proposed the following objectives: a constituent assembly, an interim constitution, an interim legislature, an interim government, local administration and policing, a democratic constitutional monarchy, the establishment of human rights and transitional justice, the management of arms and armies, and principles of social and economical transformation

(CPA Article, 2006; Crisis Group, 2006). The CPA also brought the Maoist rebels into the political mainstream (Pokhrel, 2015).

Comprehensive Peace Accord and Truth and Reconciliation Commission: The Peace Process

The peace process is divided as CPA and TRC in Nepal. They are:

Comprehensive Peace Accord of Nepal:

The Comprehensive Peace Agreement (CPA) signed on 21 November 2006 between the Nepal Government and the Maoists committed all signatories "to create an atmosphere where the Nepali people can enjoy their civil, political, economic, social and cultural rights and ... to ensuring that such rights are not violated under any circumstances in the future" (CPA Article 7.1.2). This includes political-economy and social transformations in the development of country as well as in peace building (CPA, 2006).

The CPA 2006 states in its preamble that its aim is "Reaffirming full commitment towards the 12-points Understanding, the 8-points Agreement reached between the Seven Political Parties and the Communist Party of Nepal (Maoist) (CPN Maoist), the 25-points Code of Conduct agreed between the Government of Nepal and the CPN (Maoist), the decisions of the meeting of high level leaders of the Seven Political Parties and the CPN (Maoist) held on November 8, 2006 including all agreements, understandings, code of conducts concluded between the Government of Nepal and the CPN (Maoist)".

The CPA committed to end the war and establish long term peace in the country. As it states in the End of War section:

6.2 The decision taken by the meeting of high level leaders of the Seven Political Parties and the CPN (Maoist) on November 8, 2006 shall be the main policy basis for long term peace.

According to the CPA, the interim government established the Interim Constitution Draft Committee in 2007. It consisted of Nepalese experts in constitution, democracy and parliamentary laws who were appointed by the interim government and drafted the Interim Constitution of Nepal 2007 (ICG, 2007). This was the first step in the peace process following the CPA. The Interim Constitution and its amendments established a federal state with a president, as head of state to replace the monarch and a transition from a Hindu state to a secular one. The interim constitution provided for formerly marginalised groups to be represented on a proportional basis in the new political and state institutions (Tamang, 2012).

The CPA was also crucial in developing other agreements such as those monitoring the management of weapons of the state and the Maoist insurgents, and the establishment of the constitutional assembly election. The discussion on the monitoring and management of arms was held on 8 December 2006 in presence of the UN representative, Mr Tamrat Samuel (Whitfield, 2008). The Agreement on Monitoring of the Management of Arms and Armies (AMMAA) was signed by the Maoist leadership and the Government on 26 Nov 2006 and was witnessed by the UN representative Ian Martin. This agreement gave the UN oversight in the monitoring the management of weapons and was a guarantee for the fundamental right of Nepalese people to live in peace and to vote in the Constituent Assembly (CA) election *(www.southasiaanalysis.org)*. Temporary 28 cantonments were built for 19,602 former Maoist combatants (People's Liberation Army) in southern Nepal and were monitored by the United Nations Mission in Nepal (UNMIN) until the former combatants were integrated into society and the Nepal Army (GTZ, 2010). In total, 17,052 insurgents actually participated in this UNMIN and the Army Integration Special Committee (ASISC) process for the verification. 1,444 Maoist combatants were incorporated into the national Army while 15,602 ex-combatants voluntarily "retired" (Upreti, 2011; Shah, 2012; Hamal, 2013; Subedi, 2013). Although only a few Maoist combatants were incorporated into the Nepal Army, it was an achievement of the peace process. After the cease fire agreement, most of the Maoist insurgents voluntarily retired and were given a cash payment (Subedi, 2013). Officially, the formal process of integration and reintegration was concluded in 2013.

Another fundamental aspect of the CPA program was the first election of a constitution assembly with First-Past-The-Post (FPTP) method which was held on 10 April 2008. The Maoist party candidates won 220 out of the 606 places on the assembly. This represented the largest number of places of any of the parties in the assembly (Newman, 2008). For the first time, this constituent assembly was to draft a constitution in Nepal (CCD, 2009). However, the constitutional assembly failed to deliver a new constitution and was dissolved because of political differences over the delineation of a federated state, which included questions around identity politics and communal tensions (Hachchethu, 2014). Another constitutional assembly election (II) was held on 19 November 2013 to prepare a new constitution. In this election, "... the Nepal Communist Party (Maoist) remained in the third position with 26 seats under the FPTP category" (NEOC, 2013, p.43).

The CA (II) established five committees on Friday, 28 March 2014 to expedite the drafting of a new constitution. They were divided into the Constitutional Political Dialogue and Consensus Committee, the Constitution Documents Study and Determination Committee, the Constitution Drafting Committee, the Civil Relations and Constitution Suggestion Committee, and the Capacity Enhancement and Resources Management Committee (Gorkhapatra, March 29, 2014; Ranjitkar, 2014). Disagreement over issues relating to federalism, such as the number, name and demarcation were not resolved (Tiwari, 2014). In the mean time on 8 June 2015, the major four political parties- NC, UML, UCPN (Maoist) (United Communist Party of Nepal) and Madhesi People's Rights Forum (Democratic) finally struck a deal on post monarchy constitution drafting, deferring some of the contentious issues to be decided later. Ending years of political uncertainty, they agreed to federate the country into eight provinces and promulgate a constitution, leaving the issues of names to be decided later by a two-thirds majority of the state assembly of respective provinces. They also agreed to form a Federal Commission to delineate the boundaries of the federal provinces; of the 30 parties in the alliance, 17 different parties as well as the Rastriya Prajatantra Party (Nepal) and the fractions of Maoist party were against these decisions so was not passed by the constituent assembly (Setopati, 2015).

Truth and Reconciliation Commission in Nepal:

The establishment of TRC in Nepal was a long process. According to the CPA 2006, Article 5.2.5, the TRC was to be established (Government of Nepal, 2006) in 2007. Despite the CPA advocating for a TRC, various political power struggles, Nepal's culture of impunity, the rejection of international criticism terming it as foreign interference, and the military contravening the Supreme Court orders have delayed its establishment (Anderson, 2014).

The evolution of Nepal's TRC has been described as:

The genesis of the Truth and Reconciliation Commission is less clear. Some fairly close observers were surprised to see the provisions for a truth commission in the CPA, not having heard of extensive discussion on the subject. Moreover, a senior advisor to the peace secretariat noted that there was no mention of a TRC in the first four drafts of the CPA. However, national members and international advisors to the peace secretariat recalled that forming a TRC had been informally discussed by both the peace secretariat and its task force. This discussion was initially fuelled by the interest of the [National Congress party] members of the government in forming a long-term mechanism to address past violations— which they assumed had been largely committed by the Maoists. In the beginning, the Maoists did not easily accept the suggestion to form a TRC, maintaining that the names of the disappeared should first be published. (Farasat & Hayner, 2009, p.20)

The summit meeting on 8 November 2006 was the first to mention a high-level commission to investigate disappearances (Torne, 2013) and a TRC. According to this summit agreement:

I.2 A high-level commission shall be constituted to investigate and make public the whereabouts of citizens reported to have been disappeared by the State and the Maoists in the past.

IV.4 A high-level Truth and Reconciliation Commission shall be constituted on the basis of consensus for establishing the facts on those involved in gross violation of human rights and those who committed crimes against humanity in the course of the armed conflict and for creating an environment of reconciliation in society.

The commitment to resolve questions surrounding the disappeared was set out under the heading "Situation Normalization Measures" in the "Ceasefire" section:

5.2.3 Both sides agree to make public within 60 days of the signing of the agreement information about the real name, caste and address of the people 'disappeared' or killed during war and inform the family about it.

5.2.5 Both sides agree to set up a High-level Truth and Reconciliation Commission through mutual agreement in order to investigate truth about people seriously violating human rights and involved in crimes against humanity, and to create an environment of reconciliation in the society.

7.1.3 Both sides express the commitment that impartial investigation and action would be carried according to law against people responsible for creating obstructions to the exercise of the rights envisaged in the letter of agreement and ensure that impunity will not be tolerated. Apart from this, they also ensure the right of the victims of conflict and torture and the family of disappeared to obtain relief.

7.3.2 Both sides, fully respecting the individual's right to freedom and security, will not keep anyone under arbitrary or illegal detention, commit kidnapping or hold captive. Both sides agree to make public the status of every individual "disappeared" and held captive and inform about this to their family members, legal advisors and other authorized people.

The Interim Constitution of Nepal 2063 (2007) obligated the government to set in place a relief program for the families of victims of enforced disappearance. According to Interim constitution 2007, article 33, the responsibilities of the state in the sector of TRC included:

(p) To make arrangements for appropriate relief, recognition and rehabilitation for the family of the deceased persons, the disabled and helpless persons due to injury during the course of armed conflict.

(q) To provide relief to the families of the victims on the basis of the report of the Investigation Commission constituted to investigate the cases of disappearances made during the course of the conflict.

(s) To constitute a high-level Truth and Reconciliation Commission to investigate the facts regarding grave violations of human rights and crimes against humanity committed during the course of conflict, and create an atmosphere of reconciliation in the society.

In June 2007, a decision of the Supreme Court of Nepal ordered the government to enact special laws to criminalize enforced disappearance, to form a commission to determine the whereabouts of disappeared persons, and provide interim relief to victims' families (Writ No. 3575, Supreme Court decision (June 1, 2007); none of these were implemented. In May 2007 the Ministry of Peace and Reconstruction formed a Working Group mandated to draft legislation necessary to establish a TRC according to CPA 2006, Article 5.2.5.(Amnesty, 2007) A Bill "The TRC Bill" was made for making provisions relating to Truth and Reconciliation Commission and was finalized in July in the same year. Similarly, the act was also prepared as TR Act 2007 (TRC Act 2064, section 3, 27).

Around the same time, in mid-2007, the Ministry of Peace and Reconciliation (MoPR) circulated a first draft of a Truth and Reconciliation Commission (TRC) Bill, 2064 (2007). Under that draft legislation, the TRC was to examine human rights violations that had occurred between 13 February 1996 and 21 November 2006 (TR Act, 2007). The commission was to have the power to recommend amnesties if the perpetrator submitted an amnesty application showing regret for "the misdeeds carried out" during the armed conflict (ibid). A person who was "found to have committed gross violation of human rights or crime against humanity" could receive an amnesty recommendation if those crimes were committed "in course of abiding by his/ her duties or with the objective of fulfilling political motives." Although the amnesty provision had caveats that amnesty could not be recommended for murder, inhumane treatment, torture, or rape, their inclusion created enormous mistrust and resistance among civil society and victims' groups (Amnesty, 2007; ICTJ, 2011).

The language on amnesties in the first draft, and future variations reflects the text of the legislation that established the South African TRC (Promotion of National Unity and Reconciliation, 1995) but in a simplified manner, omitting the requirements set by the South African law for the consideration of an amnesty petition. In particular, the South African law is meticulous in the definition of what a "political objective" may be and what conditions could become grounds for an amnesty; these definitions were not included in the Nepali TRC drafts.

In November 2008, a Maoist-led government made public a bill on Enforced Disappearances (Crime and Punishment), and then issued it unilaterally as an ordinance in 2009 while parliament was in recess.

Nonetheless that ordinance expired before implementation, due to a lapse of time. Various additional drafts of separate bills on a Commission on Investigation of Disappeared Persons (CIDP) and a TRC followed, but none became law. According to the proposed TRC Act-2008, its aim was to investigate the truth about grave human rights violations, bring the facts to the public, bring the perpetrators of such incidents to justice, rehabilitate and compensate victims of such crimes, end impunity, ensure that such acts did not happen again in the future, and prepare an atmosphere of peace and reconciliation by encouraging goodwill, cooperation and fraternity between the perpetrators and victims. The process of establishing a TRC in Nepal was begun as per the provision in Article 5.2.5 of the Comprehensive Peace Accord through the "Truth and Reconciliation Commission Act". Similarly a parallel commission related to the Truth and Reconciliation Commission but more specifically dealing with the finding of disappeared individuals was provisioned for in Article 5.2.3 of the CPA. The time duration was provisioned to be two years from the date of the creation of the commission which could be extended by one year (NSNM, 2011).

In August 2012, the President promulgated an ordinance on the recommendation of the Council of Ministers as there was no legislature- parliament, pursuant to sub-clause (1) of article 88 of the Interim Constitution of Nepal 2007. This promulgation was to establish a "Commission on the Investigation of Disappeared Persons, Truth and Reconciliation," and to merge the functions of both the TRC and the COID (Ordinance-8, 2013). This combined approach suffered from the "the same critical problems from the original bills and in some aspects, like the amnesty provisions, worsened them" (ICTJ, 2014, p.82). Civil society advocates resisted the move and litigated before the Supreme Court against its implementation, citing constitutional grounds (Supreme Court order 069-WS-0057, 2013).

On 14 March 2013, President Ram Baran Yadav passed an ordinance creating a TRC. On 1 April 2013, the Supreme Court suspended the ordinance from taking effect Commission due to numerous problems with the mandate and the structure of the Commission (ijrcenter.org, 2013).

In 2013, ordinance was again given to establish the CIDP and TRC. The Ordinance invoked considerable criticism from Office of the United Nations High Commissioner for Human Rights (UNOHCHR), (OHCHR, 2012, 2013) national and international NGOs (Human Rights Watch,

2013) for its failure to comply with international legal standards and was in part, struck down by the Supreme Court of Nepal in January 2014 (Supreme Court, 2014). In its judgement, the Supreme Court ordered the establishment of two commissions, on truth and reconciliation and on enforced disappearances, with the enactment of new laws to exclude the possibility of amnesty for serious human rights violations and the criminalization of serious human rights violations as specific offences within domestic law (ibid).

On 25 April 2014, more than seven years after the People's War, the Supreme Court of Nepal passed a decree to establish the TRC (Anderson, 2014) that was first proposed in 2006. The Bill was presented to and passed by Nepal's Parliament for the Commission on Investigation of Disappeared Persons, Truth and Reconciliation Act 2014.

The Commission on Investigation of Disappeared Persons, Truth and Reconciliation Act 2014 is Nepal's latest attempt to establish a transitional programme to respond to conflict and human rights abuses that occurred during the People's War. In part, the Act remedies the inadequacies of the 2013 Ordinance. It creates two commissions, on truth and reconciliation and enforced disappearances, makes provision for the establishment of a Special Court to try past abuses and incorporates systems to enable vulnerable witnesses to participate in truth seeking (Bisset, 2014). According to this Act-2014, the commission has powers:

> ➤ To find out and publish the incident of the grave violation of human rights committed in the course of the armed conflict between the State Party and the then Communist Party of Nepal (Maoist) from 13 February 1996 to 21 November 2006 and of the persons involved in those incidents upon realizing the essence and spirit of the Interim Constitution of Nepal, 2007 and the comprehensive peace accord

> ➤ To create an environment conducive for sustainable peace and reconciliation by enhancing spirit of mutual good faith and tolerance in the society upon bringing about reconciliation

> ➤ To provide for reparation to the victims

> ➤ To make recommendation for legal actions against those who were involved in the serious offence related with those incidents.

The CIDP and TRC Act, 2014, under Section 13, stipulate the functions, duties and powers of the Commission as follow:

➢ Investigate incidents of gross violations of human rights, find out and record the truth and public it for the general public.

➢ Identify victims and perpetrators of conflict.

➢ Endeavour to bring about reconciliation between the victims and perpetrators with their consent and bring about reconciliation.

➢ Make recommendation on reparation and/or compensation to be provided to the victims and their families.

➢ Make recommendation for legal action against perpetrators to whom amnesty is not granted and in cases where reconciliation is not reached.

➢ Provide the victims with identity card as prescribed and also provide them with information after completion of investigation.

The term "gross violation of human rights" is defined in section 2 (j) of the CIDP and TRC Act, 2014 as follows:

"Gross violation of human rights" means the following acts committed during the conflict targeted against unarmed person or civilian population or the following acts committed in a systematic manner:

➢ Murder,

➢ Abduction and taking of hostage,

➢ Enforced disappearance,

➢ Causing mutilation and disability,

➢ Physical or mental torture,

➢ Rape and sexual violence,

➢ Looting, possession, damage or arson of private or public property,

➢ Forced eviction from house and land or any other kind of displacement, and

> ➢ Any kind of inhuman acts inconsistent with the international human rights or humanitarian law or other crimes against humanity.

In February 2015, the long awaited TRC and CIDP in Nepal were finally formed nine years after signing the Comprehensive Peace Accord (CPA), but upon shaky grounds. Section 22 gave the TRC powers to mediate between the victims and the perpetrators on the request of either party - the perpetrator or the victim. In addition, Section 26 stipulated that "the Commission shall not recommend for amnesty to the perpetrators involved in rape and other crimes of serious nature in which the Commission follows the investigation and does not find sufficient reasons and grounds for amnesty." Therefore, the Commission could recommend amnesty for all crimes under its jurisdiction if sufficient reason and grounds were found. These provisions have now been annulled by the Supreme Court on 26 February 2015. This is a promising step forward in the delayed process of recognition of the victim's concerns (Jha, 2015). The commissions are expected to deliver victim-centric justice but such outcomes remain undecided. In the nine months since being established, interaction programs on the activities of the TRC with representatives of Government offices, civil society and journalists, and conflict victims have been undertaken in 20 of 75 districts in Nepal, and separately conducted by the office bearers of the Commission (TRC, 2016).

According to CPA-2006, the peace process was to complete three major tasks; reintegrate the Maoist ex-combatants, construct a federated secular state and draft a new constitution (Subedi, 2013). Of these tasks, only the reintegration of the Maoist ex-combatants had been achieved by 2015. The other tasks remain unaccomplished despite nine years passing since the signing of the CPA.

Successive post-2006 governments have failed to win the Nepali people's confidence (Bhatta, 2013). The 12 point understanding has, paradoxically, only deepened the instability and uncertainty in the country (Ghimire, 2012). Points like a new constitution, construction of a federated secular state, development of the country's political economy and the Nepalese people's welfare have been bypassed in the peace process (Marquette & Beswick, 2011). Bhatta (2013) states, there has been a remarkable increase in other countries' influence on Nepalese politics after the insurgency and the palace coup. As a result, current Nepali political leaders are influenced especially by India (Muni, 2012). India provides scholarships to the children of political leaders including the Maoists (Irrespective of their competency) as well as those of high profile bureaucrats and, civil society elites; they will act in India's interests in Nepal (Bhatta, 2013). No current political parties and/or leaders are focussed on the peace process in Nepal and at present the parties involved in the peace process are unwilling to find any resolution to the ongoing problems through negotiation. There should be a comprehensive outline to guide and enact an egalitarian peace-making process. The unstable Nepalese government is unable to maintain peace in Nepal and the negotiations of the peace process are protracted if not paralysed.

Scholarly research has examined the causes and effects of the conflict in Nepal but the peace process and/or why it remains unfinished as well as the role of institutions like TRC has been little examined. This thesis identifies the peace process in Nepal as a gap in the existing scholarly research. This study attempts to examine the role of TRC for social peace and the peace process in Nepal from case studies of S. Africa, Liberia and Sierra Leone. It suggests a more suitable and acceptable role for the TRC in the peace process for the future of the Nepali people which is essential for a permanent peace and social betterment.

CHAPTER 4

An overview of the Truth and Reconciliation Commission in the Peace Process

Introduction of the TRC

Throughout history, people of the world have been inflicted and witnessed atrocities against one another. In response, international governments have demonstrated a preference for war tribunals such as those at Nuremberg in Germany following World War II. After the 1950s, the retribution and war tribunals shifted toward truth and reconciliation commissions to facilitate restorative justice with this shift being most common among transitional governments (DeMinck, 2007). The first such commission was Argentina's National Commission on the Disappearance of Persons, created by President of Argentina Raúl Alfonsín on 15 December 1983 that documented human rights violations under the military dictatorship. The report was delivered to Alfonsín on 20 September 1984 and opened the door to the Trial of the Juntas, the first major trial held for war crimes since the Nuremberg trials, and the first to be conducted by a civilian court (El Pais, 1985).

Since 1973, more than 20 "truth commissions" have been established around the globe with the majority, 15 in number, created between 1974 and 1994 (Avruch & Vejarano, 2001). The term "truth commission" has come to be generally applied to bodies that officially investigate a past pattern of abuses (Hayner, 2001) while the term "truth and reconciliation commission" is a recently developed notion that has gained popularity based on the South African Truth and Reconciliation Commission (ibid). Truth commissions are different from other forms of transitional justice as they have certain characteristics that make them unique. These include i) focusing on the past and the future instead of the present in the potential development of the society; ii) investigating a pattern of abuses over a particular, defined period of time, rather than a specific event or a state's entire history; iii) are temporary in nature, most typically lasting only six months to two years; iv) culminate in the submission or publication of a report documenting its findings; and v) are officially sanctioned, authorized, or empowered by the newly formed and developing state, and occasionally also, by the armed opposition if such an arrangement is negotiated in the peace or transition agreement (Hayner, 2001).

In the history of TRC, the naming is dependent on the country's circumstances as well as the functions of it. TRCs in different countries have had different name and functions. For example;

Table 4.1 The TRC from different countries with functions

S.N.	Country	Name of TRC	Functions
1	Argentina	National Commission on the Disappearance of Persons (*Comisión Nacional sobre la Desaparición de Personas*)	Investigating the human rights violations, forced disappearances
2	Brazil	The non-punitive National Truth Commission (*Comissão Nacional da Verdade*)	victims or people accused of violations
3	Canada	The Indian Residential Schools Truth and Reconciliation Commission	investigating the human rights abuses
4	Colombia	The National Commission for Reparation and Reconciliation (*Comisión Nacional de Reparación y Reconciliación*)	help victims to recover from the armed conflict
5	Chile	The National Truth and Reconciliation Commission (*Comisión Nacional de Verdad y Reconciliación*)	investigating deaths and disappearances

S.N.	Country	Name of TRC	Functions
6	Czech Republic	The Office for the Documentation and the Investigation of the Crimes of Communism (*Úřad dokumentace a vyšetřování zločinů komunismu*)	investigating criminal acts from the period 1948-1989
7	Ecuador	The Truth Commission (*La Comisión de la Verdad*)	investigating the violation of human rights
8	El Salvador	The Commission on the Truth for El Salvador (*Comisión de la Verdad para El Salvador*)	investigating murders and executions committed
9	Fiji	Reconciliation and Unity Commission.	Investigating the human rights violations
10	Ghana	National Reconciliation Commission	Investigating the human rights violations
11	Guatemala	Historical Clarification Commission (*Comisión para el Esclarecimiento Histórico*)	Investigating the human rights violations
12	Haiti	The Haitian National Truth and Justice Commission.	Investigating the human rights violations
13	Kenya	Waki Commission; The Truth, Justice and Reconciliation Commission of Kenya	Investigating the human rights violations
14	Liberia	Truth and Reconciliation Commission	Investigating the human rights violations
15	Morocco	Equity and Reconciliation Commission (IER)	Investigating the human rights violations
16	Nepal	Truth and Reconciliation Commission	Finding truth and helping in reconciliation
17	Panama	Truth Commission (*Comisión de la Verdad*).	Investigating the human rights violations
18	Paraguay	Truth and Justice Commission (*Comisión de Verdad y Justicia*).	Investigating the human rights violations

S.N.	Country	Name of TRC	Functions
19	Peru	Truth and Reconciliation Commission *(Comisión de la Verdad y Reconciliación)*.	Investigating the human rights violations
20	Poland	Institute of National Remembrance.	Investigating the human rights violations
21	Philippines	Philippine Truth Commission of 2010	Investigating the human rights violations
22	Sierra Leone	Truth and Reconciliation Commission.	Investigating the human rights violations
23	Solomon Islands	Truth and Reconciliation Commission (Solomon Island)	Investigating the human rights violations
24	S. Africa	Truth and Reconciliation Commission	Investigating the human rights violations
25	S. Korea	Truth and Reconciliation Commission	Investigating the human rights violations
26	Sri Lanka	Lessons Learnt and Reconciliation Commission.	Investigating the human rights violations
27	East Timor	Commission for Reception, Truth and Reconciliation in East Timor *(Comissão de Acolhimento, Verdade e Reconciliação de Timor Leste*; 2001–2005); Indonesia–Timor Leste Commission of Truth and Friendship (2005–2008).	Investigating the human rights violations
28	Tunisia	Truth and Dignity Commission (2014)	Investigating the human rights violations
29	Uganda	Uganda Commission of Inquiry into Violations of Human Rights (1986-1994)	Investigating the human rights violations
30	Ukraine	Ukrainian National Remembrance Institute	Investigating the human rights violations

(Source: Robert & Thompson, 2000)

Most commissions have been named Truth and Reconciliation but some have not. Czech Republic, for example, named the commission "The Office for the Documentation and the Investigation of the Crimes of Communism", Guatemala the "Historical Clarification Commission", Poland the "Institute of National Remembrance", Sri Lanka the "Lessons Learnt and Reconciliation Commission", Uganda the "Uganda Commission of Inquiry into Violations of Human Rights" and in the Ukraine the "Ukrainian National Remembrance Institute" (Table No. 4.1).

The term truth and reconciliation commission has increasingly been used to generically describe all truth commissions (Hayner, 2001). Some scholars argue however that the term is misleading and inaccurate because many truth commissions have not held "reconciliation" as a primary goal of their work and have not assumed that reconciliation would result. Reconciliation has been an explicit goal in several truth commissions (Chile, South Africa, Peru, and Sierra Leon), an implied goal in most others, and deemed "impractical and unattainable" in a few states (Argentina and Sri Lanka) (Connolly, 2006). However, some sort of reconciliation or restorative truth-finding has been central to the majority of these bodies and has been used as a justification for implementing a truth commission instead of other types of transitional justice (ibid). In fact, the possibility of holding a truth commission is often one of the terms discussed and brokered in the peace negotiations leading up to societal transitions (Hayner, 2001). A truth commission is not however, a substitute for formal justice. Rather it is a complementary initiative (CIDA, n.d.). As such a truth commission is one of the larger programs of justice that is widely perceived as essential and important for effective peace building in a transitional or post-conflict environment of a country.

Truth commissions are generally established to investigate a past history of violations of human rights in a particular country. These might include violations by the military, other government forces or armed opposition forces/ rebellions. Generally, a truth commission is established soon after the governmental transition in order to aid this process because with the passage of time witnesses and evidence will only become more difficult to find (Migyirka, 2008).

Truth commissions can be established by different types of authorities. Sometimes they are created by the new executive branch of government or by an executive order of the state's President (Bronkhorst, 2006), for example, the National Commission on Truth and Reconciliation in Chile was created by presidential decree and completed its work in 1990-1991. In other states, such as South Africa, the country's legislative body voted to establish the truth commission which worked from 1995 to 1998 (ibid). Still other truth commissions have been created under the auspices of an intergovernmental organization, such as the UN in El Salvador (1992-1993) and Guatemala (1997-1999) (ibid).

The usual philosophy behind establishing a TRC is a belief in the healing power of truth, as a tangible report of the history of abuses is published and disseminated widely for people to understand (Aning & Jaye, 2011). It is considered that a massive violation of human rights is more than a crime - it is an abuse of human dignity therefore it needs resolution that the courts alone cannot provide. The TRC process therefore contributes to finding justice for the victims and their families by publicly admitting the atrocity in all its detail while allowing room for those involved to give their testimony and help them move forward. It is when truth is acknowledged and justice is sought that reconciliation within a society can occur (Clark, 2008).

The concept of reconciliation adopted by TRCs is that ultimately, reconciliation is the work of civil society, not the government or the courts. As such, there is no defined format that truth commissions must follow; the committees can conduct closed-door interviews, or public hearings, which everyone can attend. There can be a formal courtroom-like atmosphere, or a much more casual, informal setting resembling a round table discussion. Further, and unlike a court of law, the truth committee accepts the victims' story as truth without requiring further inquiries or evidence, or conducting thorough investigations into each case brought before them (Migyirka, 2008).

In the most general sense of the term, a TRC is an official body set up to investigate a pattern of past human rights abuses (ibid) and mandated to produce a formal record of past violations of humanitarian and/or human rights law committed by a previous regime and/or non-state actor(s) in a defined period of recent passed time. A TRC holds that the exposure of the truth regarding human rights abuses, as perpetrated by the previous regime, may help to psychologically heal the victims and their families of such abuses and assist with the process of reconciliation (Laakso, 2003). It is only after psychological healing takes place that previously warring parties can come together in a spirit of reconciliation (Mendeloff, 2004). Reconciliation, meaning the bringing together of previously opposing parties, is a recognized means of reckoning with state-sponsored atrocity (Sarkin & Daly, 2004), the success of which might be measured by an overall feeling of peace amongst a nation's citizens (Gentilucci, 2005).

Although TRCs investigate the past, they are as much about looking forward as back because they are part of an attempted social transformation to bring about a more peaceful society in the near future. They complement, but do not substitute, courts of law, and primarily, they focus on the most serious human rights violations such as "disappearances," extra judicial and summary executions, and torture (CIDA, n.d.). Tina (1995) points out that truth commissions are usually established by transitional governments who have replaced repressive regimes after a period of widespread violence, state terror, or ethnic conflict. Transitional here is in the case of democracy and rule of law. Hayner (2001) adds that after war nothing less than a focus on the future peace and democracy of a country is needed. This can be facilitated through the impartial and good work of a TRC although the extent of their success can be limited, for example, while societal reconciliation is an often-professed goal of truth commissions, it is almost always beyond the reach of a TRC on its own (Brahm, 2004).

Many legal institutions can play a central part in dealing with past atrocities in newly established democracies. Besides criminal trials, TRCs have become a frequently used tool to investigate past human rights abuses (Hayner 1994). Although they are not the institutions of law enforcement, most have quasi-judicial functions. For example, the most sophisticated TRC to date, the South African Truth and Reconciliation Commission, can be compared with a court that cannot pass sentence, but can grant or refuse amnesty to perpetrators of gross human rights violations (Theissen, 1999). Instead of making recommendations for prosecution, a truth commission does not normally have the power to prosecute. Usually, a TRC does not even identify the witnesses. Often, the perpetrators of the abuses can be granted amnesty by a truth commission. Consequently, there can be a conflict between finding the truth and administering justice. The ability of a truth commission to conduct and complete its mission successfully depends on the resources at its disposal (Brahm, 2004).

Characteristics and objectives of the TRC:

Effective truth commissions are based on certain principles and possess core characteristics that are common across all contexts. The three major principles on which truth commissions are based are:

> ➤ They are considered a neutral enterprise by all stakeholders.

> ➤ They conduct their activities impartially.

> ➤ They only focus on past abuses and violations (CIDA, n.d.).

Similarly, TRCs have four main goals:

> ➤ They seek to contribute to transitional peace by creating an authoritative record of what happened;

> ➤ Providing a platform for the victims to tell their stories and obtain some form of redress;

> ➤ Recommending legislative, structural or other changes to avoid a repetition of past abuses; and

> ➤ Establishing who was responsible and providing a measure of accountability for the perpetrators (Popkin & Arriaza, 1995).

Most truth commissions produce a public report containing information gathered from victims, and in some cases perpetrators, as well as recommendations to enhance justice and reconciliation (Bronkhorst, 2006). Additionally, many truth commissions are created to examine relatively recent events or a period of events ending in the recent past; usually occur at the point of or just after a full-scale political transition; typically investigate politically motivated acts, such as politically targeted human rights abuses and repression that was used to obtain or maintain political power and discourage potential political challenges; and examine widespread abuses, usually including thousands of cases or a large section of the state's population (Hayner, 2001). Many truth commissions are also intentionally designated to be a central feature of the state's transition program from one form of government to another or from a period of violence, such as civil war, to a period of peace (ibid).

In history, the majority of truth commissions have been established by the national government of the affected country. A number of other bodies have also been created to serve similar functions of investigating past human rights violations. In some instances, NGOs have created their own truth commissions where governments have failed to create one. The Archbishop of Sao Paulo, for example, with the support of the World Council of Churches, investigated human rights abuses under Brazil's military regime when the government refused to act on their calls for a formal inquiry (Brahm, 2004). Further, truth commissions need not be national in scope. The Greensboro Truth and Community Reconciliation Project in North Carolina created a TRC in May 2004 to examine racially motivated killings by the Ku Klux Klan and the American Nazi Party in 1979 (Magarrell & Gutlerrez, 2006).

Some "Commissions of Inquiry" with "Truth and Reconciliation" commissions are as follows:

Table 4.2 The TRC from different countries with their dates and some references

S.N.	Country	Established in	Sponsored by	Reference
1	El Salvador	1992-1993	UN	
2	Rwanda	1993	NGO	
3	Paraguay	1976	NGO	
4	S. Africa	1992	African National Congress (ANC)	During anti-Apartheid struggle
		1993	ANC	
		1995	Parliament	After Apartheid, report in 1998
5	Argentina	1983-1984	Government	Published in UK and USA too
6	Bolivia	1982-1984	Government	Disbanded without issuing a final report
7	Uruguay	1985	Government	
8	Zimbabwe	1985	Government	Report never publicly released
9	Chile	1990-1991	Government	
10	Chad	1991-1992	Government	

S.N.	Country	Established in	Sponsored by	Reference
11	Germany	1992-1994	Government	
12	Guatemala	1997-1999	Government	
13	Haiti	1995-1996	Government	
14	Nigeria	1999	Government	
15	Philippines	1986	Government	Report never completed
16	Sierra Leone	1999	Government	
17	Uganda	1974	Government	
		1986-1995	Government	
18	Brazil	1986	Government	
19	East Timor	1999-2000	Government	
20	Ethiopia	1993-2000	Government	
21	Honduras	1993	Government	

(*Source: Hayner (1994, 2001), Kritz (1995), Popkin (2000), Popkin and Roht-Arriaza (1995)*

The sense of justice facilitate is one of several forms of "transitional justice" often employed soon after a nation has changed governing regimes, most often from some form of tyranny to some form of democracy.

Different TRCs have been mandated for different durations of time to run and complete their task throughout the history. Some of them are as follows:

Table 4.3 The TRC from some countries with their duration

S.N.	Country	Duration
1	Argentina	2 years
2	Bolivia	2 years
3	Chad	1 year and 5 months
4	Chili	9 months
5	El Salvador	8 months
6	Peru	2 years and 1 month

S.N.	Country	Duration
7	Rwanda	Since 1999 to present
8	Ghana	1 year and 9 months
9	Haiti	11 months
10	Liberia	3 years and 4 months
11	Nigeria	2 years and 11 months
12	Sierra Leone	2 years
13	South Africa	7 years
14	Timor-Leste (East Timor)	3 years and 9 months
15	Uruguay	2 years

(Source: USIP, 2011)

Functions of the TRC

To achieve its objectives, a TRC shall:

➤ Facilitate, and where necessary initiate or coordinate, inquiries into:

- gross violations of human rights, including violations which were part of a systematic pattern of abuse;

- the nature, causes and extent of gross violations of human rights, including the antecedents, circumstances, factors, context, motives and perspectives which led to such violations;

- the identity of all persons, authorities, institutions and organizations involved in such violations;

- the question whether such violations were the result of deliberate planning on the part of the State or a former state or any of their organs, or of any political organization, liberation movement or other group or individual;

- accountability, political or otherwise, for any such violation;

➤ Facilitate, and initiate or coordinate, the gathering of information and the receiving of evidence from any person, including persons claiming to be victims of such violations or the representatives of such victims, which establish the identity of victims of such violations, their fate or present whereabouts and the nature and extent of the harm suffered by such victims;

➤ Facilitate and promote the granting of amnesty in respect of acts associated with' political objectives, by receiving from persons desiring to make a full disclosure of all the relevant facts relating to such acts, applications for the granting of amnesty in respect of such acts, and transmitting such applications to the Committee on Amnesty for its decision, and by publishing decisions granting amnesty in the Government Gazette;

➤ Determine what articles have been destroyed by any person in order to conceal violations of human rights or acts associated with a political objective;

➤ Prepare a comprehensive report which sets out its activities and findings, based on factual and objective information and evidence collected or received by it or placed at its disposal;

➤ Make recommendations to the President with regard to:

- the policy which should be followed or measures which should be taken with regard to the granting of reparation to victims or the taking of other measures aimed at rehabilitating and restoring the human and civil dignity of victims;

- measures which should be taken to grant urgent interim reparation to victims;

➤ Make recommendations to the Minister with regard to the development of a limited witness protection programme for the purposes of the Act;

➤ Make recommendations to the President with regard to the creation of institutions conducive to a stable and fair society and the institutional, administrative and legislative measures which should be taken or introduced in order to prevent the commission of human rights violations.

(Greiff, 2006)

Truth and reconciliation commissions, unlike trials and historical commissions are the institutional models best equipped to promote reconciliation in a fractured society, if for no other reason than the fact that they are usually set up for this express purpose (Daly & Sarkin, 2001). Although criminal trials may offer a significant sense of healing and satisfaction to victims, (Goldstone, 1996), their utility for reconciliation is doubtful. In fact, reconciliation may be the antithesis of prosecution (Daly & Sarkin, 2004).

Daly and Sarkin (2004) claim that:

[T]he relevance to reconciliation of trials, generally, is questionable, but the impact on reconciliation of international trials is surely minimal. The primary reason for this is that trials that take place outside the country are likely to have little effect on relations among people within the country. Even when international trials take place within the country, as in Sierra Leone, they are, by definition, conducted by foreigners – people who were not involved in the actual events (p.723).

Moreover, truth commissions are far superior to private environs for the exchange of confession and forgiveness; as such an exchange takes place in a non-confrontational and non-dangerous environment (Schalkwyk, 2004).

The idea behind the truth commission is that after a period of severe human rights abuses, such as enforced disappearances or massacres, abductions and rape during civil war or military repression, a society needs a forum in which victims and their families, and witnesses can share their life experienced stories and begin the healing process. Furthermore, findings of truth commissions can become a permanent record of investigation, evidence and testimony that can later be used in courts and elsewhere as a reminder of the events of an era of human rights abuses (Sierra Leonean TRC, 2000).

Compositions of the TRC:

The functions of a truth commission are highly dependent on the appointed commissioners since the primary objective of such a commission is to investigate the truth and provide justice according to its mandate and to preserve the evidence relating to human rights abuses. According to Migyikra (2008), to build credible evidence, a TRC must be independent and comprise competent and credible personnel or officials if a truth commission is to have moral authority (ibid).

The issue of constructing a commission depends upon several factors like whom, who and how should commission members be appointed and what qualities they should possess. These selection criteria directly affect the functioning of a TRC hence; there are different possibilities to consider. For example, a commission can comprise solely of nationals of the country in question, as in the case of Bolivia, Argentina and Chile (Kritz, 1995). It can also be made up solely of foreigners who are well-known international figures as in El Salvador (Brahm, 2004). Alternatively, it can consist of both foreign personnel and nationals of the country in question, as happened in Haiti and Guatemala (Steiner, n.d).

Whether the committee is formed by national or international characteristics, there are advantages and disadvantages to each approach. According to Migyikra (2008), an international commission may appear to be more objective and impartial than a national commission. This is due to the distance of its members from the events and the interests at stake, usually involving the participation to varying degrees, of an international organization, such as the UN, and the fact that the terms of its mandate have also been debated under the auspices of the UN (Hayner, 1994). In fact, the international nature of a commission may alienate some sections of society, who may see the commission's activity as foreign intervention or at least use it as an argument to discredit it. A criticism is that foreign commissioners are far less likely to have the same in-depth knowledge of the events to be investigated as commissioners from the country itself (APT, n.d.). Thus, there has been less truth commissions established with international assistance (Sierra Leonean TRC, 2004).

International support can be helpful however, particularly when domestic civil society and the government is weak. The Guatemalan and Salvadoran peace accords called for truth commissions under the auspices of the UN. The government of Burundi asked the UN to set up a commission of inquiry in 1995 because it did not feel strong enough to do so itself. In some cases, an international element has been necessary in situations where the state that previously existed has disintegrated, as in the case of the former Yugoslavia (Hayner, 1994). Commissions established by national government or the civil society can experience complete or partial failure, for example, Chad, Uganda, Philippines, and Bolivia did not have the necessary human and material resources and, in particular, did not have an adequate budget (Hayner, 1994). This was not the case for international commissions set up under the auspices of the UN (Avruch & Vejarano, 2001). However, whenever possible, setting up commissions which are wholly or partly national appears to be the best solution since it is a way of encouraging those engaged in establishing the rule of law and addressing impunity to assume their responsibilities and start making decisions for them (Migyikra, 2008).

TRCs composed and established by the national government with civil society include those in Argentina, Bolivia, Chad, Ghana, Morocco, Nigeria, Peru, South Africa, East Timor and Uganda-1986. The commission of Argentina was composed of thirteen commissioners: twelve men and one woman. Of them, ten were non-legislative members appointed by President Alfonsin and three were elected by Argentina's legislative Chamber of Deputies of Congress (TRC, 1986). The Bolivian commission had an eight person panel which was headed by the Under-Secretary of the Ministry of the Interior whereas the commission's vice-president was a representative of the legislative power. The commission also included representatives from the Human Rights Permanent Assembly and the "Association of Relatives of the Disappeared Detainees and Martyrs for National Liberation of Bolivia" (ASOFAMD). It had six additional staff, Carmen Loyola Guzman, head of the ASOFAMD, was the commission's executive secretary (Hayner, 1994). The decree of Chad created the Chad's commission of ten members and two secretaries as the members of the commission of inquiry where one commissioner was female. It was chaired by Chad's Chief Prosecutor Mahamat Hassan Abakar (INSEC, 2013).

The National Reconciliation Commission of Ghana was comprised of nine Ghanian commissioners i.e.; six men and three women. It was chaired by Former Chief Justice K. E. Amua-Sekyi (Attafuah, 2004). In Morocco, the Equity and Reconciliation Commission was comprised of sixteen commissioners appointed by the king, but included only one woman. Driss Benzikri, a former political prisoner and human rights activist, chaired this commission. Five of the commissioners were former political prisoners, including two who had been exiled (Amnesty, 2004). The Human Rights Violations Investigation Commission in Nigeria was comprised of eight commissioners where six men and two women. It was headed by Justice Chukwudifu Oputa and all the members were appointed by the President (Lamb, 1999). The Peru TRC was comprised of twelve Peruvian commissioners which included ten men and two women, and chaired by Salomon Lerner Febres. All the members were appointed by the President with the approval of the Council of Ministers. The commission opened five regional offices to carry out its work (Cuya, 2008).

According to Amnesty report (2009), the South African TRC was comprised of seventeen commissioners where nine men and eight women were participated. Anglican Archbishop Desmond Tutu chaired this commission. The commissioners were supported by approximately 300 staff members, divided into three committees as Human Rights Violations Committee, Amnesty Committee, and Reparations and Rehabilitation Committee (Amnesty, 2009; Boraine, 2000). The East Timor commission was comprised of seven members of five men and two women. It was divided and included twenty-nine regional commissioners. A lawyer and human rights activist Aniceto Guterres Lopes chaired the commission (CAVR, n.d.). The Commission of Inquiry into Violations of Human Rights of Uganda in 1986 was comprised of six commissioners, all male, and chaired by Ugandan Supreme Court Justice Arthur Oder (Quinn, 2004).

Commissions established with international support were El Salvador, Haiti, Liberia, Sierra Leone, and Uganda in 1974. The commission of El Salvador was comprised of three international commissioners, all men, appointed by the Secretary-General of the United Nations. The commission was chaired by former Colombian president Belisario Betancur (Thomas, 1994). Another commission composed of international persons was the Haiti TRC. This commission was composed of seven members with five men and two women, including four Haitians and three internationals. It was chaired by Haitian Sociologist, Fracoise Boucard (Amnesty, 2004).

The Liberian human rights activist and environmental lawyer Jerome Verdier chaired the Liberian commission which consisted of nine commissioners of four women and five men. A three-member International Technical Advisory Committee was provided for by the TRC Act i.e.; nominated by the Economic Community of West African States (ECOWAS) and the UN high commissioner for human rights (TRC Act, 2006). Sierra Leone's TRC comprised of seven commissioners: four men and three women, of whom four were Sierra Leoneans and three were internationals. It was chaired by Bishop Dr. Joseph Humper (ICTJ, 2002). The commission of Uganda in 1974 was comprised of four Ugandan nationals who were all men. It was chaired by an expatriate Pakistani judge, and included two Ugandan police superintendents and a Ugandan army officer (Carver, 1990; Hayner, 1994).

Immunity, Power and Rules of Procedures of the TRC

Most truth commissions have had the powers they needed to carry out their mission established, to some extent, through a series of guarantees contained in the enabling legislation (ICTJ, 2014). These guarantees include immunity for commissioners and protection for commission files, the power to request reports and testimony related to the investigations undertaken and the power to request or adopt preventive measures, either to protect victims or witnesses or to safeguard evidence (ibid). The most far-reaching powers existed in the South African TRC, where the Commission's report had concrete legal consequences in terms of whether the individuals investigated were amnestied or prosecuted (Hayner, 1994).

The guarantees or the powers are important in determining if the commission can produce positive results, even in the most difficult situations. During establishing the investigative powers of any commissions, considerations should be given to contextual factors and situations. The Sábato Commission for example, had to do a great deal of its work abroad, receiving testimony from victims living outside of Argentina who, despite the return to constitutional government, had decided to remain in exile because they did not feel safe in their country (Cuya, 1999).

In order to carry out the functions entrusted to it, a truth commission needs to have some common powers. These include:

➤ The power to summon persons, including government officials, to appear before the commission and to produce articles or documents.

➤ The authorization to conduct inspections in places of interest, such as prison facilities and military barracks, and initiate exhumations in accordance with the law and in coordination with law enforcement.

> ➤ The authorization to obtain official cooperation to ensure the security of proceedings, offices, and persons related to the commission (Gonzalez, 2013).

However, power is not enough to carry out the tasks of commissions because members of the commission, staff, and persons cooperating with the inquiry must be protected against physical threats or any kind of reprisal resulting from their work or participation. In Ghana, the commission was guaranteed which reduced the possibility of frivolous legal harassment (Ghana TRC, 2002). Similarly, The East Timor mandate provided fairness guarantees, though they were not exhaustive. Some other guarantees have included the right to legal representation for defendants or the right to respond to allegations or adverse findings (Gonzalez, 2013).

Resources of the TRC

In order to complete their task, TRCS must be granted sufficient resources or funds. But for many transitional states, it is difficult to access and/or manage the resources. Consequently, in many cases, the truth commissions have faced shortages of resources. Some however have not, for example, the South African TRC had a staff of 300 and a budget of $18 million per year for its two-and-a-half year existence (S. African TRC, 1999). The South Korean commission was reported to have 240 staff members and an annual budget of US$15-20 million (Dong-Choon & Selden, 2010). On the other hand, Chad's truth commission had to establish its office within the former secret detention centre of the security forces due to limited space and resources (Brahm, 2004).

In the case of Uganda in 1987, the Ford Foundation donated US$93,000 to the Ugandan government to allow the commission to continue its work. Despite other international donations, the truth commission faced continuous financial problems further delaying its work (Weaver, 2016). According to a recommendation of the TRC in Paraguay, approximately 400 individuals received financial compensation totalling US$20 million but the lack of resources was a major problem throughout the commission's work, especially in its early stage when the Paraguayan parliament cut its budget by half. In December 2007, the government stopped the funding of the commission and it had to suspend investigations for several months (Florentin & Manuel, 2006).

The Equity and Reconciliation Commission of Morocco, the first truth commission in the Arab world, distributed US$85 million to approximately 16,000 individuals who were victimised at the end of 2007 (Amnesty, 2004). Rwanda which is another country that respected the truth commission's recommendation of reparation had to depend completely on foreign governments for the annual budget of UD$300,000 (Fombad, 2008).

Reports of the TRC

The most important task of a commission is to publish the report with its findings and recommendations. According to Brahm (2004), the commission's final report is its legacy. It is a summary of the key findings. Patterns of abuse are outlined. Most importantly, the commission's report provides recommendations for rebuilding society.

Recommendations often centre on judicial, military, and police reform. The commission of Ghana recommended reforms within the prisons, the police and the military (Ghana National Reconciliation Commission, 2004). Likewise, the Nigerian commission recommended the fragmentation of the police system (Nigeria Human Rights Violations Investigation Commission, 2002).

Importantly, the Truth commissions also make recommendations for reparations to victims. Although this compensation is incomparable to the suffering the commissions can recommend reparations as a different means to healing wounds for the families of the disappeared, continuing prosecutions and for follow-up investigations concerning persons who remain missing (Argentine National Commission on Disappeared, 1984). In 2004, $3 billion was provided for the reparations to victims in Argentina. The report on El Salvador indicated the reparations for victims included memorials and monetary compensation (Naidu, 2004). A comprehensive reparation program, including apologies, a memorial, and monetary compensation was recommended by the Ghana commission. For this, the amount paid to victims was to be based on type violations suffered for approximately 3,000 victims of repression under Rawlings' rule (Ghana NRC, 2002).

Although, every report includes adequate investigations and solid conclusions, some of the most valuable reports, and the conclusions within it, have been somewhat brief, as in Argentina, while in others – Chile, Guatemala or even Haiti – they have been lengthy (Avruch & Vejarano, 2002). However, According to Mygikra (2008);

> It should not be forgotten that the most important thing is the dynamic aspect of a report in terms of what impact it will have on society and whether or not justice and reparations will follow it. It is also important for the report to provide the impetus for reform of the State, and especially of the justice system and the armed and security forces and police, so that democracy and the rule of law can be established on solid foundations (p. 45).

The truth commission can make a specific proposal about follow-up in its report as in Haiti (Hayner, 2001). For example, it might propose a specific body to be set up or entrusted to a national human rights commission such as the Ombudsman's Office or the National Human Rights Commissions. The question of follow-up has been given greater attention in the reports of some recent commissions such as the CEH in Guatemala and the Commission of Inquiry in Sri Lanka (Popkin, 1999).

Looking at the different types of truth commissions that have been established, most of the commissions worked for a limited timeframe, although those of Chad and Uganda are to run for an indefinite period (Sarkin & Daly, 2004). The commission's terms of reference may allow it to look at a pattern of abuses over a number of decades (Chile and South Africa), or instead focus on specific crimes or specific groups of perpetrators (ibid) where some revealed the identities of perpetrators as in Timor-Leste and some did not as in Chile, Guatemala (Pathak, 2016). However, some attempted a massive exercise in public participation and mobilisation like in South Africa, Sierra Leone whereas other commissions are smaller and more secretive like in Guatemala, Sri Lanka, Haiti (Rotberg, 2000). Similarly, some commissions have had broad powers of subpoena, search and seizure as well as to make recommendations, whilst others do not have (Sarkin & Daly, 2004; Stahn, 2001). Indeed, the truth commission is a flexible institution, capable to adapt different national circumstances.

It is very much important to have appropriate rules regarding procedure and evidence to guide the investigations and all other tasks of a TRC so that all circumstantial, documentary and material evidence available can be properly used meaningfully and appropriately. For this, the commissions should have experienced staff in gathering documentary evidence, particularly as Truth commissions seek to collect evidence from a variety of sources such as taking witness statements and inspecting sites including detention centres, mass graves, etc (Brahm, 2004; Migyikra, 2008). This requires good relationships and cooperation between different bodies like government, military, police, human rights commission, courts, and victims as well as perpetrators. Sometimes, for a particular investigation, a researcher will be assigned to investigate; once their investigations are completed, findings are presented to a panel. Then the panel will decide for further investigation or finalization. Usually everything relating to rules of procedure and evidence is detailed within the working rules, regulations, and mandates of the commission (Migyikra, 2008).

CHAPTER – 5

Case Study of the Liberian Civil War and Truth and Reconciliation Commission

Background of the Conflict

Liberia is located on the Atlantic coast of West Africa and comprises an area of 43,000 square miles. Liberia has a population of approximately 3.3 million and its neighbours are Sierra Leone to the northwest, Guinea to the northeast, and Côte d'Ivoire to the southeast. Historically, 15 counties, each claimed by particular indigenous ethnic groups made up Liberia. English is the official language however more than 20 indigenous languages are in daily use. Although it is a country rich in natural resources like timber, gold, diamonds and rubber, Liberia is a low human development country, ranking 177th in the world (HDR, 2016).

Liberia's political history is replete with conflicts. During the pre-colonial period, there were many conflicts and wars frequently occurred between Liberians from 1822 to 1847. Liberia became a sovereign country under Americo-Liberian rule in 1847 but continued to face conflicts about border legitimacy, inclusion and identity, land, and a struggle for supremacy (Liberian TRC, 2009). Between 1822 and 1867, more than 13,000 freed slaves were sent to Liberia (Bascom, 2009). For 133 years Liberia was rules by a small elite composed of Amrico-Liberians, freed slaves of African descent from slave ships known as 'Congos' (Ojielo, 2010) who settled in Monrovia, Liberia's capital in 1822. They comprised only five percent of the total population but they dominated the majority indigenous populations and the government, economy, security, commerce and social advancement.

Between the 1800s and mid 1900s, Liberia developed into a stable oligarchy (Foster et al (2009). Over 100 years, the Americo-Liberian political party, the True Whig Party, ruled Liberia. In 1943, William V.S. Tubman, an Americo-Liberian, became President and ruled until his death in 1971. During the Tubman presidency, 3.5per cent of the Liberians held 60per cent of the nation's wealth while the rest lived in extreme poverty (Liberian TRC, 2009). After Tubman, William R. Tolbert became President; Tolbert's rule, like his predecessor's, was marked by a further exclusion of indigenous representation in government. In April 1979, riots involving about 2000 people broke out and escalated in the capital city, Monrovia. The riots, known as the 'rice riots' because they were triggered by hunger, were suppressed. The following year, an army master sergeant and an Indigenous-Liberian, Samuel Doe led a group called the 'People's Revolutionary Council (PRC)' and attacked then President Tolbert and key members of cabinet. The President was killed in this attack. Samuel Doe took power and became Liberia's new national leader. This event ended 133 years of settler oppression and began the era of Indigenous rule (Dolo, 1996).

Under Doe's rule, many injustices took place (Foster et al, 2009). These included the public execution of most of the officials of the Tolbert government, alignment – then evaporation of Liberia's relationship with the United States of America (USA), a fraudulent election in 1985, and atrocities on his own ethnic group in 1990. The construction of a range of government ministries was one of Doe's achievements, with his ethnic politics marking the beginning of civil war in his period of nepotism and corruption (africanarguments.org, 2015). Doe was enriching himself (Abiodun, 1998:10) and his nationalism gave way to ethnocentrism and military repression (Nass, 2000), leading to further division in the country, further decline of the Liberian economy, and even lower living standards for the majority of the population (Harsh, n.d.).

Charles Taylor was half Liberian; his mother who belonged to ethnic group in Liberia had earned a degree in the USA (Burlij, 1977). Taylor however returned to Liberia and supported the 12 April 1980 coup led by Samuel Doe. For this, he was appointed the Director-General of the General Services Agency (GSA) in Doe's government. In 1984, Taylor fled to the US amid charges of embezzling US $1 million in public funds. As Doe requested, Taylor was arrested and imprisoned in Boston. In 1985,

Taylor escaped from prison and his whereabouts were unknown (Aboagye, 1999). Later, it was discovered he had undertaken guerrilla training in Libya (Ohaegbulam, 2004).

On 24 December 1989, the National Patriotic Front of Liberia (NPFL), a rebel group of 15,000, invaded Liberia from the neighbouring Cote d'Ivoire (Adekeye, 2002). The NPFL was headed by Charles Taylor (Omonijo, 1990) and was formed with the stated objective to remove Samuel Doe from office, arguing that Liberians had suffered too long under his regime. This was the first Liberian civil war and it raged until 2003 (Cook, 2003). The NPFL encountered little difficulty and started to recruit more members, especially from among two particular ethnic groups, the Gio and Mano. Doe's regime had massacred many Gios and Manos and anyone else who opposed him, resulting in the mass murder of innocent men, women and children as entire villages were set ablaze (Ofuatey-Kodjoe, 1994). Equally disturbing were the reports of hundreds of babies and children being thrown into wells to drown after their parents had been killed (William, 2002). These groups were therefore easily recruited due to the atrocities they had suffered under the Doe regime and their desire to take revenge on Doe and his government. During the early stages of the civil war many atrocities were committed by both the NPFL rebels and on the orders of Doe.

Other internal and external factors also significantly contributed to the outbreak and continuation of the civil war. The social and economical conditions of the country such as mass illiteracy and poverty, corruption, selfishness, greed and economic disparities were major factors in the conflict. Similarly, discrimination against women and the denial of their rightful place in society as equal partners, the over centralization of power and wealth in the country and the unwise distribution of land, combined with growing disunity and ethnic rivalries, increased tensions in Liberia (Foster et al, 2009).

The U.S. Ambassador to Liberia, James Bishop, criticized the Doe government and called for an end to the hostilities. He asked the Doe government to declare a county named Nimba as a disaster zone but Doe declined the request (William, 2002). Doe continued to stand his ground; he refused to resign as the NPFL demanded and threatened that more lives would be destroyed if the NPFL did not surrender to the government. This stalemate between the fighting parties made the country more unstable.

By April 1990, five months after their initial invasion, the structure of the NPFL was beginning to fracture. Commander Price Yormie Johnson had split from the NPFL and formed the Independent National Patriotic Front of Liberia because Taylor had executed some of his soldiers for being defeated by government forces in Ganta (Aboagye, 1999). The split between Taylor and Johnson created a second war front, as both fought against each other, as well as the government. However, both rebel groups made their way toward the capital Monrovia and their forces began to weaken Doe and his government (Abrokwaa, n.d.). Over the next 12 months, Taylor rose to power, murdering Doe on 10 Sept 1990 and declaring himself President; this exacerbated the civil war in Liberia (Gerdes, 2013).

The war in Liberia also had international dimensions and trans-border repercussions. In the beginning of war, many Western African nationals were involved as fighters and many African states provided different forms of support to different actors. The African states provided support to the rebels from Libya, Burkina Faso, Cote d'Ivoire, Ghana, Nigeria, Guinea and Sierra Leone. On the other hand, Sierra Leone provided sanctuary to Liberian rebels to overthrow the Taylor regime. Additionally, other non-state actors and/or arms dealers like Victor Bout, a Ukrainian national, became involved in the war (Aning & Jaye, 2011).

The USA supported Tubman's rule of a virtual police state for 27 years and the authoritarian rule of American Colonization Society (ACS) (Wallton, 2014). This undermined Tolbert's non-alignment policy and further influenced the people to fight against the government. Similarly, despite condemnations from Congress regarding the conduct of the 1985 elections, the USA continued to recognize Doe as the legitimate leader of Liberia and continued to provide him with support (Liberian TRC, 2009, vol 2, p. 306). The USA's support of Samuel Doe Junta in Liberia in acquiring military weapons to suppress and violate human rights also motivated the rebels to fight. On all occasions and in all instances, the USA acted first and foremost to foster its economic, commercial and political interests in Liberia rather than protecting the rights of the Liberian people and enhancing their development. This made the Liberians more determined to fight against the government (Liberian TRC, 2009, vol 2, p. 308).

In 1991, the Economic Community of West African States (ECOWAS) intervened in Liberia, both diplomatically and militarily, to stop the war. Despite 14 peace accords being negotiated by the ECOWAS with the warring parties between June 1991 and August 1996 (Aning et al, 2010), the country remained unstable. In 1997, Taylor was elected President but his government faced armed opposition from several significant violator rebel groups, as shown in Table 1(Aning & Jaye, 2011).

The Warring Parties

The warring parties in Liberia during the 15 year civil war numbered more than a dozen – this is more than any other country that has suffered a civil war. The armed groups, rebel groups or warring factions and their financiers, leaders, commanders, combatants and advisors associated with and responsible for the conflict in Liberia can be categorized into three groups; significant violator groups, less significant violator groups and military institutions (Liberian TRC, 2009). They were as follows:

Table 5.1: Warring Parties in Liberia

S. N.	Significant Violator Groups
1	National Patriotic Front of Liberia (NPFL)
2	Liberians United for Reconciliation and Democracy (LURD)
3	Liberian Peace Council (LPC)
4	Militia, Movement for Democracy in Liberia (MODEL)
5	United Liberation Movement (ULIMO)
6	Armed Forces of Liberia (AFL)
7	United Liberation Movement-K (ULIMO K)
8	Independent National Patriotic Front of Liberia (INPFL)
9	United Liberation Movement-J (ULIMO J)
10	Anti-Terrorist Unity (ATU)
	Less Significant Violator Groups
1	Vigilantes
2	Lofa Defense Force (LDF)
3	Liberian National Police
4	Special Operation Division of the Liberian National Police (SOD)
5	Revolutionary United Front (RUF)
6	Special Anti-Terrorist Unit (SATU)
7	Special Security Unit (SSU)

8	Special Security Service (SSS)
9	National Security Agency (NSA)
10	National Bureau of Investigation (NBI)
11	Criminal Investment Division (CID)
12	Rapid Response Unit (RRU)
	The Military Institutions
1	Economic Community of West African States Monitoring Group (ECOMOG)
2	Black Beret

Source: Aning & Jaye, 2011; Liberian TRC, 2009

Consequences of the Conflict

The lengthy civil war had many consequences for the country. The massive and flagrant human rights abuses led to the death of more than 250,000 people and the collapse of the state and society. The United Nations/Office of the High Commissioner for Human Rights (UN/OHCHR) Assessment Mission to Liberia (2007) reported that the human rights situation in Liberia was extremely precarious on several fronts. The major issues were widespread poverty and lack of food security, massive unemployment, no access to health care and education, few basic services and a collapsed economy. The civil war disrupted livelihoods, disintegrated state structures, shattered the economy and unbalanced cultures, traditions and religions. People fled their homes and families separated as poverty increased and they became vulnerable to predation, hunger, disease, rape, sexual abuses and abduction (Mission to Liberia, 2007).

Twenty-three types of human rights violations were recorded and among them forceful displacement accounted for 36 percent which made the people refugees and 2.5 million were displaced (Liberian TRC, 2009, p. 282; BBC, 2009). It is estimated 60 to 70 per cent of the population suffered some form of sexual violence (BBC, 2009). Men were the major victims, accounting for 47 percent of all violations. Many women and girls were sexually assaulted by gender-based violations such as rape, sexual slavery and sexual abuse which accounted for 28 per cent of all violations (Advocates for Human Rights, 2009, pp. 9-11). Abduction, assault, forced displacement, killing, looting, torture, forced recruitment and forced labour were also common. Barbaric practices like eating the enemy's heart or blood to strengthen the conqueror also developed among the warring combatants (Liberian TRC, 2009). One of the most harmful long-term aspects of the conflict however was the recruitment and use of child soldiers (Deng, 2001).

The country was also abused and exploited. Liberia's timber forests, diamond mines, infrastructure and telecommunications were ransacked. For example, the University of Liberia granted 284,000 acres of its forest to an offshore company (Oriental Trading Company) for US $2 million but the payments were never made (Liberian TRC Report, 2009, p. 290). Roads were damaged and destroyed and the hydro-electric plant which provided electricity to Monrovia and its environs, but never to villages, was deliberately vandalized. Similarly, the water treatment plant was also damaged. Public offices and facilities including ministries, agencies, sport stadiums, radio stations, hospitals, and systems experienced were significantly damaged and rendered ineffective (ibid, 2009).

The Liberian Truth and Reconciliation Commission:

After 15 years of war in Liberia, a special court indicted former Liberian President Doe and the warlord Charles Taylor. A comprehensive peace agreement (CPA, 2003) was signed between the government of Liberia and the Liberians Unite for Reconciliation and Democracy (LURD) and the Movement for Democracy in Liberia (MODEL) and political parties in Accra, Ghana on August 18, 2003. Within the framework of the ECOWAS peace process for Liberia, the different parties and people who had pursued peace throughout Liberia's civil war were well represented (Steinberg, 2009, p. 137). The Accra agreement called for the establishment of an independent national commission on human rights, and the creation of a TRC. The signing of the comprehensive peace agreement thus opened the way for the establishment of a TRC in Liberia under the general outline of the TRC's mission, as included in Part Six, Article XIII of this Peace Accord (Accra, 2003; ICG, 2009). As such the Commission was tasked with investigating and addressing the root causes of the crisis in Liberia, including human rights violations (Comprehensive Peace Agreement, 2003).

Background of the Establishment

Before the enactment of the TRC Act in Liberia, during May 2005, a process of national dialogue, consultation and consensus building took place. According to the Liberian TRC report (2009), on January 4, 2004, Chairman Bryant constituted a nine member TRC panel of commissioners. This panel failed to gain legitimacy in the country however. Thereafter, a conference was convened on April 29, 2004, and the Liberian TRC proposal document was circulated on August 13, 2004. The TRC Act was signed into law on June 10, 2005 and published into a Bill on June 22, 2005. The Liberian TRC was inaugurated on February 20, 2006.

Initially, the TRC was established with a working plan for October 2005 to September 2008. The Commission could not complete its task of finding the root causes and consequences of conflict to inform recommendations and procedures for reconciliation and reparation. Hence, it was extended by 10 months, until June 30, 2009 to complete its task (Liberian TRC Report, 2009).

The Objectives/ Role of TRC in Liberia

The TRC was established by the government of Liberia, according to the Accra Peace agreement, to enquire into the human rights violations that occurred in Liberia from 1979 to 2003 (Ojielo, 2010). Its overall objective was to promote national peace, security, unity and reconciliation (Article IV Section 4, TRC Act of Liberia 2005). It was mandated to identify the accountability of possible persons, authorities, institutions and organisations involved in the civil war (Liberian TRC Report, Vol. 1). It was also specifically established to provide a forum that will address issues of impunity, as well as an opportunity for both the victims and perpetrators of human rights violations to share their experiences and reconciliation in order to create a clear picture of the past so as to facilitate genuine healing and reconciliation (3, Article III, Comprehensive Peace Agreement, 18 August 2003).

The TRC in Liberia was empowered to investigate human rights violations and economic crimes under the TRC Act and to promote national healing and reconciliation (Long, 2008). The Commission was to investigate violations that occurred in between January 1979, the final year of the Americo-Liberian rule, and October 2003, the day of the inauguration of the National Transitional Government of Liberia (Lansana, 2015; Ycaza, 2013). It was also to investigate the root causes of the conflict and adopt mechanisms and procedures to address the experiences of vulnerable groups such as women and children through its recommendations and measures for the rehabilitation of victims of human rights violations, reconciliation, and reparation as part of healing (NTLA, 2005). The human rights abuses of massacres, sexual violations, murder, extra-judicial killings as well as the economic crimes like the exploitation of natural resources to perpetuate armed conflicts during 1979 to 2003 were determining areas of the TRC in Liberia so that impacts on victims could be determined for reconciliation, rehabilitation and reparation (Liberian TRC Act, Section 4, 2003).

The TRC was also responsible for gathering information from victims, perpetrators, witnesses and institutions through public and confidential hearings (Long, 2008). This task played a vital role in terms of providing opportunities for everyone to be heard and in in restoring the human dignity of victims. In special cases, the TRC had the mandate to recommend amnesty under terms and conditions if international laws and standards had not been violated (Liberian TRC Act, 2003).

Preparing and compiling a comprehensive report was another important task of the TRC in Liberia (Jaye, 2009). The report included findings and recommendations based on the information collected. The recommendations to the Head of State were on a range of issues including reparations, making findings and determinations on all matters brought before the Commission and adopting its own rules (Ojielo, 2010). The recommendations were in specific areas - legal institutional and other reforms, continuing investigations and inquiries, and prosecutions (Liberian TRC Act, Article VII, Sec, 26 (j), 2003).

The Structure/ Composition of the TRC

Liberia had one TRC committee and one Advisory committee for the peace process. According to Comprehensive Peace Accord (CPA), Article XIII, the head of the National Transitional Government of Liberia, Charles Gyude Bryant nominated nine commissioners in October 2005 to form a Liberian TRC (ICTJ, 2010, p. 5). The team of commissioners was composed of four women and five men from Liberia. The Commissioners were inducted into office by Ellen Johnson-Sirleaf, the President of Liberia, on 20 February 2006. The active phase of the TRC's two-year mandate was launched at a public ceremony in Monrovia at the Centennial Memorial Pavilion (Steinberg, 2009; TRC, 2009). According to the Liberian TRC Act (2003), all TRC Commissioners had equal powers with the Chairperson exercising his/her powers as a "first among equals". All members of the Commission could exercise oversight responsibilities for the functioning of the Commission to maintain a balanced and comprehensive perspective of TRC operations yet they were not involved in the day-to-day operations of the Commission.

Article V Section 10 of the Liberian TRC Act provides the authority to form a three-member International Technical Advisory Committee (ITAC), as nominated by ECOWAS (two members) and the UN High Commissioner for Human Rights (one member). The three member advisory committee was formed in Liberia in 2006 then 2008. The ITAC advisors provided legal and policy oversight and advised the TRC Commissioners. They were accorded the same rights and privileges as Commissioners, except the right to vote (Liberian TRC, 2009, p. 36). However, none of the commissioners had any previous experience of working with a truth commission or with transitional justice mechanisms (Gberie, 2008, p. 457).

Table 5.2: The Structure of Liberian TRC

TRC Committee	Advisory Committee
Commissioners- 9 (Women-4 and Men-5 From Liberia)	Members- 3

Source: Liberian TRC, 2009

Findings of the Liberian TRC

The TRC of Liberia released the final report and summary in four volumes on 19 December 2008 followed by the final and edited version of the report on 3 December 2009 (James-Allen et al, 2010). The findings can be divided into two sections, the causes of the 15 year long civil war and its consequences for Liberia.

The major root causes of the conflict were attributed to poverty, greed, corruption, limited access to education, economic, social, civil and political inequalities; identity conflict; land tenure and distribution (Transparency

International, 2006; The law offices of Dorsey and Whitney, 2007). Other contributors were the lack of reliable and appropriate mechanisms for the settlement of disputes and the duality of the Liberian political, social and legal systems which polarized and widened the disparities between settler Liberians and Indigenous Liberians (Consolidated Final Report, 2008, vol. 2, p. 16). The report identified one of the most disturbing and dangerous historical antecedents to the Liberian civil war was the politicization of the Liberian military (Liberian TRC, 2008, vol.1). It also found all the factions were responsible for abuses and that external state actors in Africa, North America, Europe and the USA participated, supported, aided, abetted, conspired and instigated violence, war and regime change for political, economic and foreign policy advantages and gains (Consolidated Final Report, vol. 2, p.18).

Recommendations of the Liberian TRC

The Liberian TRC worked for three years and four months and made recommendations in different sectors. The major remedial activities recommended by the TRC focused on specialized psychosocial and other rehabilitation services, legal, institutional and other reforms. The need for continuing investigations and inquiries into particular matters and the need to hold prosecutions in particular cases at the discretion of the TRC were other recommendations. The Commission's recommendations focused on establishing accountability for human rights violations. To facilitate this, the National 'Palava Hut' was established as a mechanism to foster peace dialogues and rebuild broken relationships to promote national reconciliation. This traditional justice and reconciliation processes enabled matters of concern to be resolved amongst or between individuals and/or communities. Palava Huts were especially common in rural communities around Liberia due to the lack or absence of courts, resources, lawyers, penal institutions and police officers (Liberian TRC Report, 2009). The TRC recommendation was to establish this system in all statutory districts for not less than three years but not more than five years.

The TRC recommended the establishment of the "Extraordinary Criminal Court for Liberia" to prosecute 124 key individuals for gross human rights violations. These included violations of international humanitarian law, international human rights law, war crimes and economic crimes including, but not limited to, killing, gang rape, multiple rape, forced recruitment, sexual slavery, forced labour, exposure to deprivation, and abduction (Liberian TRC Report, 2008, Vol. II). It recommended prosecuting eight leaders of warring factions and 116 notorious persons, including Charles G. Taylor. The TRC also recommended these persons be barred from holding public office for 30 years as a form of sanction. Similarly, the TRC recommended 45 persons be prosecuted for economic crimes, barred from holding public office for 30 years and all the assets they had acquired unlawfully during the conflict were seized.

The TRC further recommended 58 individuals who had committed egregious domestic crimes, but lesser than gross violations, be prosecuted under the jurisdiction of the domestic criminal courts (Liberian TRC Report, 2008, vol. 2). The TRC also recommended that 38 individuals should be pardoned from prosecution for co-operating with the TRC, expressing their remorse, and confessing to crimes they had committed (Ycaza, 2013). The TRC found 49 government officials, including President Ellen Johnson Sirleaf, guilty of committing gross human rights violations, international humanitarian law violations, war crimes and egregious domestic law violations due to their roles during the civil war and instability in Liberia between 1979 and 2003. The TRC recommended these persons be subjected to public sanctions to fulfil the purpose to promote integrity in public service and restore confidence (Article VII Section 26 (a) (b) (c) (d) (e), Liberian TRC Act, 2005). They should not be appointed in the government or legislative authority or have power to govern or make decisions on behalf of the Liberian people whom they victimized. For those holding elective public offices, the TRC allowed them to continue to the end of their tenure however they were banned from holding any public office in the future for a period of 30 years from 1 July 2009. Those holding appointed offices had to resign immediately (Liberian TRC Report 2008, vol. 2, p. 360). Unfortunately, this recommendation was criticized and ignited debate over peace versus justice because Sirleaf was a key actor in bringing peace to Liberia. However, the public sanctions were to provide a form of justice and demonstrate accountability, redress impunity, and promote integrity in public service (Liberian TRC Report, 2008, vol. 2, p. 360).

Importantly, the TRC recommended some reparation procedures. These included the establishment of a Reparations Trust Fund of approximately US $ 500 million over 30 years. The fund would be utilized for compulsory free education from primary to secondary education and college level across subjects such as medicine, nursing, teacher training, agriculture, science and technology. The fund also provided help for mental and physical health such as psychological, physical, therapeutic and counselling treatments. Funds were also directed to economic programs like lending schemes and small business management to women through commercial banks; infrastructure and community development projects including the establishment and re-building of schools, health facilities, and roads. The TRC further recommended reparation procedures through the establishment of a national memorial and unification day to memorize the dead and respect the survivors; the promotion and protection of the rights of women and children; and issuing a public apology to the Liberian people for the devastating civil war and loss of human life and destruction of properties in Liberia (Liberian TRC, 2009).

The TRC also made recommendations to the government of Liberia, the Liberian Diaspora and the international community. The recommendations to the government included confirming their responsibilities, duties and obligations relating to building a new Liberian political and civil culture. These included the administration of justice, the establishment and resourcing of the independent national human rights commission (INHRC), combating corruption, institutionalizing good governance and economic empowerment and poverty reduction. The recommendation to the Liberian Diaspora was to contribute at least US $1.00 per month to the Reparation Trust Fund to help the reparation process in their motherland (Liberian TRC, 2009, p. 396). Similarly, the TRC recommended international communities such as the UN Security Council, foreign states, international institutions, donors and NGO partners to continue their assistance to sustain the peace in Liberia.

Lastly, the TRC recommended different sectors to come together as a national integration of Liberian society and to form a new model of social engineering (national visioning) that would inform the rebuilding of institutions and infrastructure, media and national Bar association, amnesty, use and management of land and other natural resources, distribution and reform of land, and a commission on Liberian history (Liberian TRC, 2009).

The Liberian TRC: Strengths and Limitations

The Liberian TRC achieved mixed results. It successfully met its mandate of investigating and determining the responsibility for gross human rights violations as well as examining the root causes of the violent civil war. It was successful in providing recommendations to the Liberian government for peace and justice. Unfortunately, it did not address all the causes and consequences for peace building because of the limited budget, personnel and time covering its hearings and the lack of suitable methods of implementing its recommendations.

The Commission put forward reforms for legal and institutional laws and regulations. It was successful in recommending compulsory free education from primary level to secondary education as well as technical education such as nursing, teaching, and agriculture to help reduce the limited access to education and minimise poverty. It was also successful in decreasing the greed, corruption, civil and political inequities. The commission successfully addressed the economic causes of conflict as it recommended economic programs such as lending to small business for women and policy and program options to address these key conflict issues (Ycaza, 2013).

The Commission recommended the establishment of the 'National Palava Hut Forums' as a means of promoting justice and reconciliation at the local level. The process was based on traditional dispute resolution mechanism and was popular with the people as local elders played a role in settling matters such as extramarital affairs, divorces, land disputes, debt, and occasionally theft and murder (Pajibo, 2008, pp. 16-18). Under the aegis of the Independent Human Rights Commission, the Palava Huts provided a public venue for victims to confront perpetrators living in their communities and facilitate reconciliation between individuals, groups and communities. Traditionally, the process sought confession of the wrongful act, apology for the wrong committed, and forgiveness from the victim, followed by cleansing rituals and restitution (Pajibo, 2008, pp. 18–19). This was a critical recommendation to foster reconciliation at the local level (Liberian TRC Report, 2008, vol.3, p.2). As reconciliation takes a long time and despite the end of the war, ethnic animosities and resentments were and are still strong in the country. The establishment of a Reparations Trust Fund was another success of the commission in Liberia. It recommended to providing approximately US $ 500 million to the victims through this fund over 30 years as the reparation process.

A success of the Commission was its proposal of a general amnesty for all child combatants. This respected international law and practice and included gross human rights violations, war crimes and economic crimes as well as killing, gang rape, multiple rape, force recruitment, sexual slavery, forced labour, exposure to deprivation, and declared missing (Liberian TRC, 2009, vol 2, p. 349).

The Commission found that all warring parties in the conflict, including the state security, were responsible for human rights violations and none of the parties took any measures to control the human rights violations. The civil war to liberate the people from tyrannical rule brought only more brutal violations and oppression. The Commission recommended the establishment of a criminal court to determine the criminal responsibility of individuals and armed groups for the violations that occurred. This was to provide the justice for the victims who suffered from the criminal acts of the perpetrators.

The Commission recommended that all individuals admitting their wrongs and speaking truthfully before it as an expression of remorse should not be prosecuted and be granted amnesty. This recommendation was in keeping with the Act establishing the Commission that amnesty could be offered to those who testified truthfully and expressed remorse. But the Commission was unsuccessful in determining and verifying the minimum condition of truth when judging statements made by alleged perpetrators which raised doubts about the level of truthfulness (Transitional Justice working Group, 2008); the lack of a measurement of remorse to decide whether it was genuine and the lack of knowledge of the role of the victim or of the victim's family undermined the decision of whether to offer amnesty or not (Ojielo, 2010). In reality, a number of those recommended for amnesty were accused of gross human rights violations. The Commission did not offer any rationale or explanation for this decision of amnesty.

The Liberian TRC recorded more violations than any other TRC. According to the TRC report (Liberian TRC Report 2008, vol.2, p.185) there were 86,647 victims and 163,615 violations which were identified through the victims' statements. As a result, it was crucial to the transitional justice process that these violations be addressed through specific recommendations. The commission was unsuccessful in achieving this (ICTJ, 2010, p. 15; Steinberg, 2009); many recommendations were quite vague and not directed towards specific actors (Section 18 and 22, Liberian TRC, 2008).The commission was also criticized for lack of a due process in formulating the recommendations (Weah, 2012).

The commission failed to collect information on violations from all parts of the country (Ojielo, 2010), meaning large number of victims were excluded. The hearings were conducted in areas with available hotel accommodations for the commission members and staff and the presence of broadcast media. Hearings were thus limited to easy locations such as the administrative capital of the district or region. Therefore, although the commission recommended justice and reconciliation, a tenuous peace existed between victims and perpetrators.

In general, due to the lack of policies on reparations and prosecutions, the work speed of the TRC in Liberia was very slow. The lack of a comprehensive program for psychological advice and support to victims and witnesses, lack of sufficient protection measures for victims and witnesses, and the lack of sufficient processes to protect the perpetrators exacerbated delays (Amnesty, 2008). These delays resulted in the TRC needing a nine month extension to conclude its work (James-Allen, Weah, & Goodfriend, 2010, p. 9).

The non-binding effect of the TRC's recommendations, because of the doctrine of separation of powers, was another weakness of the Liberian TRC (James et al, 2010, p. 10). Much of the evidence did not have supporting references which undermined the reliability of the facts the recommendations were based on. The lack of details made it more difficult to implement many recommendations. As Steinberg (2009) found, the recommendations on reparations failed to identify the preliminary beneficiaries and there was an absence of obvious criteria for determining who was accountable. Similarly, the TRC failed to capture the scenario of sexual based violence against women and their experiences and failed to collect the information of female combatants with the majority of these experiences being unrecorded (Ojielo, 2010). The link between sexual violence and gender-based violations was also weak as the TRC focused on the abuses of women but not men and boys (ICTJ, 2010).

Table 5.3: Strengths and Limitations of Liberian TRC

Strengths		
Nos.	**Causes of war addressed**	**Recommendations**
1	Greed and corruption	Responsible to duties and obligations to building a new Liberian political and civil culture, institutionalizing good governance
2	Education	Free education
3	Civil and political inequality	Reform of laws and regulations
4	Poverty	Economic empowerment, institutionalizing good governance
5	Economy	Economic programs
6	Reparation	Reparations Trust Fund, Diaspora, national memorial and unification day, public apology by the government
7	National integration	Social engineering
8	Human Rights violations	National Palava Hut, Criminal Court, amnesty, public sanction
Limitations/ weaknesses		
Nos.	**Weaknesses**	**Reasons**
1	Unaddressed violations	Lack of specific implementing agent, sufficient specificity, direction and guidance
2	Failed to collect all information	Covering of easy locations only
3	Slow functioning	Lack of process and policies
4	Binding effect of recommendations	Doctrine of separation of powers
5	Reliability of facts	Lack of details and references
6	Incomplete link between sexual and gender based violations	Failed to capture the scenario

Source: Liberian TRC, 2008

Conclusion

In conclusion, the Liberian TRC was successful in finding the root causes of the civil war and in its measures to address them such as the reformation of legal and institutional laws and regulations, compulsory education, and economic programs. The utilization of local procedures in reconciliation such as Palava Hut Forums, the distribution of cash through the Reparations Trust Fund over 30 years to the victims, amnesty for all child combatants and the establishment of a criminal court were successes of the Liberian commission. However, it was unsuccessful in explaining its rationale for granting amnesty, in providing specific recommendations to a large number of victims, and unsuccessful in collecting information from all parts of the country and all victims. The lack of supporting references and criteria for accountability, the binding effect of recommendation and slow work speed were other weaknesses of the Liberian TRC that impeded its success.

CHAPTER-6

Case Study of the Sierra Leonean Civil War and Truth and Reconciliation Commission

Background of the Conflict

Sierra Leone is a country in West Africa. It covers 27,699 square miles and is bordered by Guinea in the north-east, Liberia in the south-east, and the Atlantic Ocean in the south-west. About 16 ethnic groups inhabit the 14 districts of Sierra Leone, each with its own language and customs. Sierra Leone is a predominantly Muslim country with a population of 6.6 million (UNDP, 2016). It relies on mining, especially diamonds, for its economic base and is among the largest producers worldwide of titanium, bauxite, gold, platinum, chrome, and iron and has one of the world's largest deposits of rutile. Despite this natural wealth, it is a poor country, ranking 179th in the United Nations Development Programme (UNDP) scale (HDR, 2016).

The political history of Sierra Leone goes back to 1787 when 331 freed slaves arrived there (Kaifala, 2017). In 1789, Freetown was built as the capital of the country. After abolishing the slave trade in 1807, the British took responsibility for Sierra Leone, especially the coastal areas; 50,000 more freed slaves arrived during the next half-century and the country became a British colony (HRW, 2014). In 1898, the British attempted to further expand their power and exert their rule over the sovereignty of indigenous chiefs. They established a new tax which resulted in the Hut Tax war (Arthur, 1974). This war ended in 1905 but resistance continued throughout the colonial period until the 1960s, most often in the forms of intermittent rioting and chaotic labour disturbances. For example, revolts against colonial rule took place around Kambia in 1931 but the British colonial forces put down the rebellion. The West African Youth

League, a political party, again mobilized the workers against the colonial government in 1938 (Fyle, 2006) and riots in 1955 and 1956 involved tens of thousands of workers (Killson, 1966).

In early 1951, educated leaders from different ethnic groups established the Sierra Leone People's Party (SLPP) and negotiated with the British the transition to eventual national independence (World Bank, 2011). In November 1951, a new constitution was drafted with a framework for decolonisation (Taylor, 2011) and provisions for Sierra Leone to develop a parliamentary system with the Commonwealth of Nations (ibid). The first parliamentary election took place in May 1957 where SLPP won and Sir Milton Margai was elected as the Chief Minister (ibid).

On 27th April 1961, Sierra Leone celebrated independence from British colonial rule (Kamara, 2011; Momoh, 2011). Sir Albert Margai was appointed Prime Minister and enacted several laws against the opposition, the All People's Congress (APC). When Sir Milton Margai died unexpectedly in 1964, as leader of the SLPP and the sitting Prime Minister, the country became unstable once again. The opposition party leader, Siaka Stevens, was elected as the Prime Minister and he established a one-party state. This resulted in riots in 1967 (Pham, 2005). In this unstable situation, the military leader of the country, Brigadier Andrew, staged a coup and became the head of the state in the same year (Sierra Leonean TRC report, vol 3A, 2004). In 1968, Stevens resumed power as Prime Minister with the aid of Brigadier General Bangura, and declared a state of emergency (Gberie, 2005).

In 1971, Sierra Leone was declared a republic and in 1978, the government, under Stevens, again became a one-party state *under the aegis of the APC (Fowler, 2004).* In 1985 Stevens retired and nominated the head of the army, Joseph Momoh, as his successor. An unsuccessful attempt was made to overthrow Momoh in 1987 by the Vice President who was subsequently hanged and more than 60 senior governmental officers were arrested. Corruption, as well as economic decay continued, until rebel Revolutionary United Front (RUF) soldiers overthrew Momoh in 1992, calling for a return to a multiparty system *(Fowler, 2004).* In 1993, the National People's Revolutionary Council (NPRC) was formed by a group of disaffected army personnel. The opposing RUF and NPRC engaged in fierce battles for control of the country and in 1994, the NPRC staged a coup against the government and took control of the capital, including the diamond rich eastern province (Lahai & Lyons, 2015).

Among the different rebel groups, the RUF targeted civilians, murdering, raping, and amputating hands, legs and arms and forcibly recruiting people. Children as young as eight years old were recruited as soldiers and girls were forced to be domestic servants or sex slaves (Human Rights Watch, 2000; Dougherty, 2004 cited in Kelsall, 2009). The RUF leaders lost their political motivation and instead fought for personal gain, robbing civilians and plundering the country's diamond mines (Bones, 2001; Sierra Leonean TRC, 2004).

In 1996, the NPRC government and the RUF signed a ceasefire and launched a Disarmament, Demobilization and Reintegration (DDR) program, especially for the rebels (HRW, 2000). At this time however, the Armed Forces Ruling Council (AFRC) overthrew the government through a military coup and the country was plunged into chaos again. That same year, a democratic presidential election took place for the first time in Sierra Leone and the People's Party candidate, Ahmad Tejan Kabbah, won with 59.4 percent of the total votes (Larry, 2002). Kabbah was ousted however by a violent military coup in May 1997 that was headed by the leader of the AFRC. After 10 months of exile, Kabbah resumed his rule but rebel forces continued their attacks in the country (Jackson & Albrecht, 2010).

In 1998, the United Nations Security Council created the United Nations Observer Mission in Sierra Leone (UNOMSL) to monitor the situation of human rights violations (UN, 1999). It was not strong enough to intervene however and in January 1999, the AFRC and RUF rebels seized Freetown and in a two week period murdered 6000 civilians and abducted 2000 children (Bones, 2001). After several unsuccessful peace negotiations, in July 1999, the rebel groups and government signed the Lome Accord with a mandate to establish a TRC for Sierra Leone and provide a blanket amnesty upon the implementation of the DDR program (Mustafa & Bangura, 2010). The RUF disrupted the DDR process however, abducting about 500 United Nations' peacekeepers, and kidnapping and killing thousands of civilians, thus hostilities re-erupted in 2000. At that time however, after years of civil war, many rebels were tired of fighting and most decided to surrender their weapons. This led to peace finally and formally, being declared in January 2002 (Hayner, 2004). The war, which had lasted from March 1991 to January 2002 and resulted in 70,000 people being killed and 2.6 million people displaced, was officially over (Gberie, 2005; Kaldor & Vincent, 2006).

In the aftermath of the civil war, a -TRC- and a UN sponsored war crimes tribunal (the Special Court for Sierra Leone) were established according to the provisions of the Lome Accord (Migyirka, 2008). The purpose of the TRC was to provide a forum for victims and aggressors during the conflict to tell their stories and help the healing process. The purpose of the Special Court for Sierra Leone was to seek justice for people who had suffered during the civil war by putting on trial those responsible for the atrocities committed during the fighting (Perriello & Wierda, 2006).

The Warring Parties

Sierra Leone experienced civil war for 11 years. Some of the members of the rebellion were native Sierra Leones and others were not. The warring parties can be divided into internal actors and external actors (Ball, 1996; TRC, 2004), as indicated in the table below:

Table 6.1: Internal and External Actors of Sierra Leonean civil war

S.N.	Internal Actors
1.	Revolutionary United Front (RUF)
2.	Armed Forces Revolutionary Council including Westside Boys (AFRC)
3.	Sierra Leone Army (SLA)
4.	Civil Defence Force (CDF)
5.	Economic Community of West African States Military Observer Group (ECOMOG)
6.	Guinean Armed Forces (GAF)
7.	United Liberation Movement for Democracy (ULIMO)
8.	Police officers - including the special security divisions (SSD)
9.	Armed Forces Revolutionary Council/Sierra Leone Army (AFRC/SLA)
10.	Minor perpetrator groups
	External Actors
1.	Libya (as discussed in 6.2.4.1)
2.	Liberia (see 6.2.4.1)
3.	Charles Taylor and the National Patriotic Front of Liberia (NPFL) (see 6.2.4.1)

4.	United Movement for Democracy (ULIMO)
5.	Economic Community of West African States (ECOWAS)
6.	Economic Community of West African States Monitoring Group (ECOMOG)

Source: Sierra Leonean TRC, 2004

Consequences of Conflict

The conflict resulted in the widespread destruction of infrastructure (homes, schools, and hospitals) and the internal displacement of almost a quarter of the population (Keen, 2005 Richards, 1998). Almost two million people were displaced and became refugees; 400,000 fled overseas and between 800,000 and 1.3 million were internally displaced (Amowitz et al., 2002, p. 214). The civil war affected almost the entire population (Burman & McKay, 2007) and was characterized by extreme violations of human rights on all sides, including mutilation, murder, and destruction of property and looting (Sierra Leonean TRC, 2004; Burman & McKay, 2007). It is estimated that 50,000 people were killed during the conflict (Bellows & Miguel, 2006, p. 394) with abductions and arbitrary detentions being other common violations during the conflict (see Table 2).

All armed groups involved in the civil war were responsible for plundering and looting in Sierra Leone. As the leaders of all the rebel groups were aware that whoever had control of the diamond mines controlled Sierra Leone (Hirsch, 2001), the civil war was concentrated mostly in and around the diamond districts (ibid). The Sierra Leone People's Party (SLPP) government also abused the death penalty to eliminate their political opponents (Sierra Leonean TRC Report, 2004, vol 2, pp. 27-29), misusing emergency powers to suppress political dissent. Many groups used child soldiers in the civil war, especially the RUF. It is estimated that between 10, 000 to 48, 000 children were forcibly recruited and forced to take drugs to reduce their inhibitions against committing violent acts (HRW, 2003; Dougherty, 2004; Burman & McKay, 2007). These acts included "cutting off villagers' hands and fingers" (Richards, 1996, p. 6), and during "drug-induced atrocities" the RUF was said to "mutilate and even sometimes to eat their victims" (Williams 2001, p. 15). After the war, and on returning to their home and community, ex-child soldiers were often excluded and remained socially isolated due to the extreme nature of their experiences (Betancourt et al., 2010; Medeiros, 2007).

In summary, 14 types of gross human rights violations were reported to the TRC as major consequences of the civil war in Sierra Leone. These violations are identified in Table 6.2.

Table 6.2: Violations reported the Sierra Leone TRC

Types of violations	Numbers
Abduction	5,968
Amputation	378
Arbitrary detention	4,835
Assault/ Beating	3,246
Destruction of property	3,404
Extortion	1,273
Forced cannibalism	19
Forced displacement	7,983
Forced labour	1,834
Forced recruitment	331
Killing	4,514
Looting	3,044
Physical torture	2,051
Rape	626
Sexual abuse	486
Sexual slavery	191

Source: Ball, 1996; Sierra Leonean TRC, 2004

The Sierra Leone Truth and Reconciliation Commission

The civil war in Sierra Leone ended with the signing of the Lome Peace Agreement on 7 July, 1999. Article XXVI of the peace agreement between the government of Sierra Leone and the rebel RUF called for the establishment of a TRC within 90 days of signing of the agreement. However, the TRC was not enacted by the President and parliament of Sierra Leone until 2000 with the final report being issued in October 2004 (International Centre for Transitional Justice, 2010).

Background of the Establishment

In June 1999, the UN High Commissioner for Human Rights offered technical assistance to help establish the Sierra Leone TRC and the President accepted the offer (HRW, 2003). Between July and December 1999, the OHCHR- organised many consultations with civil groups, government representatives and the RUF. A working group under the National Forum for Human Rights was also established and the terms of reference for the TRC drafted. These included the recommendation that the TRC should consist of both national and international commissioners as the international commissioners would be free of parochial interests and bring fresh perspectives to the commission.

The resumption of armed conflict in Sierra Leone in May 2000 disrupted the peace building process (Sola-Martin, 2009). A ceasefire was negotiated and the peace agreement was signed in Abuja, Nigeria in November 2000 with disarmament commencing in May 2001. The Security Council, the Secretary General of the UN and the High Commissioner for Human Rights again supported and encouraged the Government of Sierra Leone and an environment was created to establish the TRC among the warring parties in March 2001.

The Sierra Leone government prepared a bill and on 22nd November 2000, the Parliament of Sierra Leone passed into law the TRC Act (TRC Act, 2000; James-Allen et al, 2003). To support the adoption of the Bill, OHCHR representatives were in the country consulting different parties to prepare a detailed plan of activities (Sierra Leonean TRC, 2004). These included the selection process of commissioners, a strategic framework for a public awareness programme, research on traditional methods of conflict resolution and conflict management, and a project to first, identify violations and abuses committed during the conflict and 'map' the key incidents and second, to establish an interim secretariat for the commission. The commission consisted of three executive secretaries, 216 staff members, 21 consultants, and 14 interns, as detailed in Table 3.

The objectives/ Role of TRC in Sierra Leone

Similar to TRCs in different countries, the TRC in Sierra Leone was established to identify and address the human rights violations in the country during the civil war. As described in the Lome Peace Agreement, the TRC was to be a catharsis for constructive interchange between victims and perpetrators of human rights violations and abuses to help create and present a clear picture of the past (Section 1, Article XXVI). The principal objectives of the TRC in Sierra Leone can be discussed in three parts.

First, the TRC was to investigate the causes, nature and extent of the human rights violations/ abuses as well as international humanitarian law abuses (Sierra Leonean TRC Act, Sec. 6). It would find out whether the violations were deliberately planned by a government, group or individual. Similarly, the role of internal, as well as external factors, would be investigated and reported in full (Sierra Leonean TRC Act, 2000, Sec. 6, Clause- a).

Second, the TRC was to help restore the human rights and dignity of victims to promote reconciliation in the country. The TRC would provide a forum for both victims and perpetrators to tell their truths. Hence, the TRC would facilitate reconciliation, promote healing and work toward preventing future violations (Sierra Leonean TRC Act, 2000, Sec. 6, Clause-b).

Third, the TRC would utilise all measures available to establish and maintain peace (Clause- c). For example, it could raise funds from both governmental and non-governmental organisations. However, it had to submit a financial report to the government on a quarterly basis (Section 1, Clause 12).

The Structure/ Composition of the TRC

In May 2002, the Government of Sierra Leone proceeded with the establishment of the commission. Seven commissioners were named by President Kabbah and duly sworn into office in July 2002 (Sierra Leonean TRC Act, 2000, Article 3 (1)). Among the seven commissioners, four men and three women, four were Sierra Leoneans and three were internationals from Gambia, Canada and South Africa. The chairman was Sierra Leonean Bishop, Dr. Joseph Humper (Sierra Leonean TRC, 2004). The different backgrounds of the TRC commissioners allowed the commission to focus on different areas (Boraine and et al, 1994). For example, the lawyers sought justice, human rights figures could seek the truth, and religious leaders could promote healing and forgiveness (Dumbuya, 2003).

Table 6.3: Structure of the Sierra Leone TRC

TRC Committee	Nationalities
Commissioners- 7 (Women-3 and Men-4)	Sierra Leone- 4 Gambia-1 Canada-1 S. Africa-1
Others	
Executive secretaries-3 Staff members-216 Consultants-21 Interns-14	Sierra Leone

Source: Sierra Leonean TRC, 2004

Findings and Recommendations of Sierra Leonean TRC

The Sierra Leone TRC gathered information on the abuses committed during the civil war and made several major recommendations. The findings and recommendations are discussed below.

Findings of the Sierra Leonean TRC

The Sierra Leonean TRC presented the final report on 5 October, 2004. The report identified the major causes of the ongoing conflict and the consequences of the war between 1991 and 2002. The Sierra Leonean TRC (2004) concluded different factors, both internal and external, made the conflict inevitable. These factors included years of bad governance, greed, endemic corruption, nepotism and the denial of basic human rights. In combination, these factors created deplorable conditions and deprived the nation of its dignity and reduced most people to a state of poverty. The political elites plundered the nation's assets and the government mismanaged the country's natural resources, including its mineral riches

(Sierra Leonean TRC, 2004, vol. 2, Arts. 13-17, p. 27); government accountability was non-existent at the expense of the national good.

The TRC traced the different and diverse causes of the Sierra Leone conflict from historical antecedents in the colonial period to post-independence years, in particular, the years preceding the outbreak of violence in 1991. Prior to 1991, each regime implemented self-serving mechanisms instead of positive and progressive policies in the country (Sierra Leonean TRC, 2004). This undermined democracy and killed the rule of law, creating the potential for violence to erupt. Bad governance and institutional collapse weakened the army, police, judiciary and civil service during the post independent period between 1961 and 1991 (ibid). A culture of intolerance for the rights of others developed among the political elites who were in key decision making position (Keen, 2003; Abdullah, 1998). The government also favoured certain ethnic groups and appointed members of them in cabinet, civil service and the army. In time, this created divisions among ethnic groups and created fierce rivalries (Shearer 1997, p. 849; Sierra Leonean TRC, 2004). Ultimately, this also fuelled the civil war in Sierra Leone, especially among the youth (Sierra Leonean TRC, 2004).

The TRC also found that among the immediate antecedents to the armed conflict in Sierra Leone, major external causes were the outbreak of armed conflict in Liberia, as well as Libya, and the role played by Charles Taylor, the leader of the National Patriotic Front of Liberia (NPFL), who provided organisational oversight to the NPFL and RUF (Abdullah, 1998; Richard, 1996). A joint agenda to instigate a civil war in Sierra Leone was developed by Taylor and Foday, the leader of the RUF, in 1990 and 1991, and the insurgency was launched in Liberia in December 1989 (see Chapter 5). The Sierra Leone army failed to prevent attacks in the border area with Liberia and this also brought the civil war into Sierra Leone from Liberia via the joint plans and attacks by the NPFL and the RUF in 1991 (Sierra Leonean TRC, 2004, Vol 2).

All these factors contributed to the collapse of an effective political system, particularly during the one party rule of the APC between 1969 and 1985. The people lost all faith in the ruling class to act with integrity and to deliver basic services to the nation and population. This, in turn, led them to believe a revolutionary movement could bring positive change to the country. Hence, the resulting civil war can be seen as the final convulsion of a failed system (Reno, 1995).

Recommendations of the Sierra Leonean TRC

The TRC's recommendations from two years of work focussed on building a new Sierra Leone based on the values of human dignity, tolerance and respect for the rights of all persons. Primarily, the recommendations intended to create an open and vibrant democracy in which all Sierra Leoneans were treated equally. The Sierra Leonean TRC Report (2004) further highlighted the need to confront the legacies of dehumanization, hatred and fear by promoting tolerance, not prejudice; a need for acknowledgment, not recrimination; a need for reparation, not retribution; a need for community, not victimization; a need for understanding, not suspicion; and a need for reconstruction, not greed.

The TRC's core recommendations related to the protection of human rights, the establishment of the rule of law, improved security services, promoting good governance, fighting corruption, and protecting the human rights of youth, woman and children. The recommendations also included the promotion of regional integration and unity by external actors, accountability for the proceeds from mineral resources, the building of the national justice system, reparations, and reconciliation - including guiding principles and reconciliation activities. Other areas of focus were a national vision of going forward, archiving of commission documentation, dissemination of the TRC Report and the establishment of a follow-up committee (Conflict Management and Development Associate et al., n.d., pp.123–125; Sierra Leonean TRC, 2004).

The establishment of a National Human Rights Commission was recommended strongly by the TRC. To foster the human rights, the commission focused on and recommended that preserving human dignity be a fundamental right in the constitution. The Commission also highlighted other measures to strengthen human rights such as abolishing the death penalty, ratifying international human rights treaties, and avoiding criminal sanctions. The TRC was particularly concerned to protect the human rights of youth, women and children, viewing this as a national emergency. The TRC further recommended discrimination against women be repealed by statutory and custody laws. To support this, they recommended political parties should ensure certain quotas were met, especially in public elections to represent the government. Children would be protected through education, with failing to send a child to school until

18 years of age and trafficking, sexual exploitation and child labour being criminal acts (Sierra Leonean TRC, 2004).

The TRC recommended the establishment of the rule of law, especially on judicial services, so that civilians could access proper justice in the country. Broadening the representation on the judicial services commission and increased representation of the Bar were key recommendations in this area. Along with this, the commission recommended creating an autonomous judiciary with budgetary independence, incorporating local courts into the judicial system and establishing a public defence system. Another recommendation of the TRC (2004) was that the security service in Sierra Leone be apolitical so that no political party or the leader could influence it.

Importantly, the TRC recommended reparation procedures to promote permanent peace in the country. Activities such as apologies from all actors who were involved in the conflict and celebrating a national peace day as well as a national reconciliation day (18th of January every year) aimed to promote reconciliation. Further, the TRC recommended observing traditional and religious activities, and social and recreational activities, to play a vital role in reconciliation. The continuation of government support for trauma counselling and support for the activities of the District Reconciliation and Support Committees set up by the TRC and the Inter-Religious Council were other important recommendations of the commission (Sierra Leonean TRC, 2004, chapter 2, vol 3). The TRC also strongly recommended responding to victims' specific needs in health, education, and economically through skill training and micro credit initiatives such as a monthly pension (Sierra Leonean TRC, 2004).

Lastly, the TRC recommended the government archive all the documents for future reference and establish a follow up committee to monitor the activities of the government, according to the TRC Act and Lome Peace agreement 1999 (Sierra Leonean TRC, 2004). The follow up committee would have four representatives from civil society, including a woman and a youth, and would report quarterly and annually, for one year only (Sierra Leonean TRC, 2004).

The Sierra Leonean TRC: Strengths and Limitations

The Sierra Leonean TRC successfully completed its mandate to determine gross human rights violations and the root causes of the 11 year civil war.

Two of the most significant successes of the TRC in Sierra Leone were the establishment of a National Human Rights Commission and the public apology by President Ernest Bai Koroma in March 2010 to all women for the violations they suffered during the conflict (Dougherty, 2004b; Sierra Leonean TRC, 2004).

The TRC identified the suppression of political expression between 1969 and 1985 as a major contributor to the war and addressed this by strongly recommending freedom of expression, and in particular, equal political representation of youths and women without discrimination to help further promote a vibrant and healthy democracy (Sierra Leonean TRC, 2004).

The establishment of the Anti-corruption Commission (ACC) and broadening the campaign against corruption were other victories of the TRC that provided stronger procedures to fight against corruption (Sierra Leonean TRC, 2004). Importantly, the TRC recommended the new leaders commit themselves to the principles of leadership as committed leadership is vital for good governance and to control corruption.

The TRC was successful in recommending the establishment of a Trust Fund as a reparation mechanism (Sierra Leonean TRC, 2004). The Fund was to be utilized to offer help such as health treatment, free education to all the children of victims, skill training for small business and micro-projects. It was also to focus on specific categories of people such as amputees, children, victims of sexual violence and certain groups of war wounded (Stovel, 2006). The TRC was also successful in recommending increasing solidarity among victims and perpetrators as symbolic reparation. The adoption of new principles in the constitution for national security to help protect the country from external influences in the future was another important success of the commission.

The TRC largely failed however to communicate its purposes and procedures to the local communities (Sierra Leonean TRC, 2004, p. 161; Sawyer et al., 2007; Miller, 2010). The delays in its establishment, the shortness of time and its limited budget of severely limited its success. It could spend only one week in each province for public hearings. Moreover, although many people wanted to testify, only a small number were chosen to and only a small amount of time was allocated to them (Dougherty, 2004b, pp. 43, 44). Similarly, reconciliation efforts were largely left to the localities (ibid, p. 44). Hence, the TRC could not collect statements from many victims (Sierra Leonean TRC, 2004, p. 169).

Specifically, the TRC could not undertake comprehensive fact finding missions to establish accurate and fair accounts of history. The commission could not comprehensively outline the antecedents of the conflict or the role of major violators, as an example, the RUF bore the greatest responsibility for the war (60.5% of all violations) but the TRC was not able to take critical testimony from its members (Painter, 2009). It did acknowledge victimization officially and this began the important work of healing (Hayner, 1994, p. 607) and reconciliation to move the country beyond its tortured past (Gibson, 2006, p.410). However the TRC did not adequately focus on reconciliation due to its greater focus on the truth component (for example, investigation, details, facts, and so on) than on the reconciliation component (for example, healing, making amends, coming together, and so forth) (Park, 2010).

Lastly, the Commission failed to offer any specific and sufficient means for the funding of various schemes like health care (a complete physical and psycho-social support), education, skill training for people with disabilities, micro grants for small business, pensions, agricultural support for farming families and community and symbolic reparation. These areas of the TRC were unsuccessful.

Table 6.4: Strengths and Limitations of Sierra Leonean TRC

Strengths		
S.N.	**Causes of war which was addressed**	**Recommendations**
1.	Suppression of political expression	Freedom of expression
2.	Exclusion of society-at-large by political elites	Increase the level of representation especially of youths and women
3.	Resources exploitation	Government accountability
4.	Corruption	New Bill, a new culture of ethics and service and fight the scourge of corruption, establishment of Anti-corruption Commission (ACC), commitment of leaders, anti-corruption campaign

5.	Human Rights violations	Establishment of National Human Rights Commission
6.	Reparation	Trust Fund, helping in education, health, skill trainings, community reparation, symbolic reparation
7.	External political effects	National security
Limitations/ weaknesses		
S.N.	**Weaknesses**	**Reasons**
1.	Delayed functioning	Rules and regulations, support from government and political parties
2.	Inadequate collection of statements all in all	Short time
3.	Inadequate focus on reconciliation	Greater focus on the truth component
4.	Inadequate fulfilment of various schemes	Lack of funding

Source: Sierra Leonean TRC, 2004

Conclusion

In conclusion, the Sierra Leonean TRC was successful in finding the root causes of conflict. Additionally, it was successful in promoting accountability in government leaders towards the country and its people. The establishment of the National Human Rights Commission, Anti-corruption Commission as well as the Trust Fund were other strengths of the TRC in Sierra Leone. However, it was slow functioning and unsuccessful in collecting statements from all the victims and perpetrators. The lack of funds and short time contributed the TRC making inadequate recommendations to address key areas of need such as health care, education, agriculture, and pensions or to meaningfully promoting avenues of reconciliation.

CHAPTER 7

Case Study of the South African Civil War and Truth and Reconciliation Commission

Background of the Conflict

South Africa is the southernmost country in Africa, covering 471, 359 square miles of land with close to 53 million people making up the population. It is bounded on the south by 2,798 kilometers of coastline stretching along the South Atlantic and Indian Oceans (Central Intelligence Agency, 2015), on the north by the neighboring countries of Namibia, Botswana and Zimbabwe, on the east by Mozambique and Swaziland, and it surrounds the Kingdom of Lesotho. Its largest city is Johannesburg, the legislative capital is Cape Town, the administrative capital is Pretoria and the judicial capital is Bloemfontein. South Africa is a multiethnic society with a wide variety of cultures, languages, and religions. The population is approximately 80% black (African), 10 per cent white (European) and 9per cent people of mixed white and black descent. The constitution recognizes 11 official languages, which is among the highest number of any country in the world. Nine of these languages are indigenous - Zulu, Xhosa, Tswana, Sotho, Swazi, Venda, Ndebele, Pedi and Tsonga - and the two are of European origin, being Afrikaans and English. About 80 per cent of the population are Christian and a small number are Muslims, Hindu, Jews and followers of traditional African religions. The UNDP ranked South Africa at 119th position in its scale (HDR, 2016).

The history of conflict in South Africa dates back to the 16th century with the arrival of the first European settlers of Dutch, German and French ancestry, known as Boers, the Afrikaans' word for farmer. The gradual expansion of these new settlers, both in land and colonial powers over the next 150 years, changed into conflict, especially between the Xhosas, Zulus, and Afrikaners. In 1806, during the Napoleonic Wars, the British officially seized the Cape (where the Dutch East Indian Company first landed in 1652), to prevent further occupation by the French. Gradually, the British began to assert their rule, forcing the Boers to change their lifestyle and language, and abolishing slavery in 1834. British rule was formalized and the discovery of diamonds in 1867 and gold in 1886 spurred competition among the British, Boers and native South Africans for wealth and immigration; it also intensified the subjugation of the native inhabitants. The Boers actively resisted British encroachments but were defeated in the Boer War that lasted from 1899 to1902. The result was a Union of South Africa that operated under a policy of apartheid i.e. the separate development of the races - Boers and native, black South Africans. On 31 May 1910, the Union of South Africa became an independent state within the British Commonwealth and in 1961 the country left the Commonwealth and became the Republic of South Africa (Saunders, 2002).

While the policy of apartheid began after the Boer War between 1899 and 1902, and it was formally established when the National Party (NP) took power in 1948. In 1950, under apartheid, the population were classified by race under the Group Areas Act that segregated blacks and whites (Baldwin-Ragaven et al, 1999). In 1954, J. G. Strijdom drove apartheid legislation even further and in 1958, his successor, H. F. Verwoerd, refined and theoretically substantiated the apartheid ideology (Migykra, 2008). Until the first half of the 20th century, the conflicts or protests about apartheid were non-violent, however these changes resulted in mass protests against the government which signalled the beginning of civil war in South Africa (International Centre for Transitional Justice (ICTJ), 2009).

During this time, black resistance, under the leadership of the African National Congress (ANC), had consolidated (ARP, 1986). Mass protests against apartheid occurred and resulted in the government banning all opposition groups and organizations. This was ineffective as the resistance organizations became militant and went underground. In 1960, a demonstration took place at Sharpeville against the white government (Rees et al, 2002). The NP repressed it by killing 70 black demonstrators. In 1976, in the Soweto uprising, thousands of pupils who were demonstrating against Afrikaans being made a compulsory school subject were shot. Unrest spread throughout the country and ANC backed guerrilla warfare on military personnel and government facilities escalated in South Africa, resulting in a full police state (Heston et al, 2002; ICTJ, 2009). This situation lasted until 1989 when the last President of the old South African government, F. W. de Klerk, openly admitted the failure of apartheid policies. This opened the door to multi-party negotiations, with the first general elections held in South Africa on 27 April 1994. This resulted in Nelson Mandela being inaugurated as the first democratically elected President of the Republic of South Africa (Tutu, 1998).

The Warring Parties

The warring parties in South Africa can be divided as non-government and government groups, as shown in Table 7.1.

Table 7.1: Lists of actors in the conflict in South Africa

S.N.	Non-Government groups:
1	**PAC-** Pan Africanist Congress
2	**ANC-** African National Congress
3	**UDF-** United Democratic Front
4	**AZAPO-** Azanian People's Organisation
5	**APLA-** Azanian People's Liberation Army
6	**MK-** Umkhonto we Sizwe
7	**IFA-** Inkatha Freedom Party
8	**HCF-** Homeland security forces
9	**ROG-** Right-wing opposition groups
10	Third Force
11	**Civil society-** General people
	Government groups:
1	**SAP-** South African Police
2	**SADF-** South African Defence Force

Source: Davis, 1987; Thompson, 1995; South African TRC, 1998

Consequences of Conflict

The impacts of the civil war on the people and country of South Africa were wide spread. One of the most important pillars for the development of a country, the economy, was destroyed. Gross human violations also took place during the 34 years of apartheid rule in South Africa. In combination, these factors had an immense economic cost with 29per cent of survivors losing income as a direct result of violation (South African TRC, 1998, vol. 5, p.154). These violations were perpetrated by all the warring parties and resulted in long-term psychological, physical, social and economical problems for the people and the country (South African TRC, 1998). Repression and exploitation severely affected the mental and physical wellbeing of the majority of people due to dire socio-economic deprivation, violent state repression and intra-community conflicts. Torture and other severe mistreatments (Table 2) often caused depression, anxiety disorders and psychotic conditions (TRC, 1998, vol. 5, p. 129), resulting in the loss of independence and dignity (National Institute of Mental Health, 1998). Survivors of abuse also reported an increased risk of infectious diseases, malignancies, and heart disease from torture or prolonged arbitrary detention (Basoglu et al, 1998; South African TRC, 1998, vol 5). These physical injuries had multiple effects on the individual and on the family and community.

Table 7.2:   The major causes of psychological trauma

Rape and punitive solitary confinement	Sexual assault, abuse and harassment
Physical beating, injuries	Shot, injuries
Burnings (by fire, petrol, chemicals)	Injury by drugs, poison, other chemicals
Mutilation (including amputation of body parts, breaking of bones, pulling out of nails, hair, or teeth or scalping)	Detention without charge or trial
Banning/ banishment	Destruction of a person's house
Deliberate failure to provide medical attention in custody	Deliberate withholding of food and water in custody

Source: South African TRC, vol 1, 1998

Physical injuries and disabilities were common during the conflict in South Africa with most caused by torture, shooting by the police into demonstrating or fleeing crowds, physical attacks and beatings and/or failed assassination attempts (South African TRC, 1998, vol.5, ch.4, p.140). South Africa also experienced unique types of killing such as burning and necklace killing (Ball, 1994). The concept of necklacing originated from the Eastern Cape in early 1985 when angry residents put a rubber car tyre around the neck of a community councillor, who was accused of having links to a vigilante group, and set it on fire as revenge for 21 people being shot down by the police (South African TRC, 1998, vol 2, p. 388). Necklacing then spread to other areas of the country.

Table 7.3: Data of Burning and Necklace killing in South Africa

Year	Total political violence deaths	Necklace/ Burning
1984	175	3/3
1985	922	67/28
1986	1352	306/84
1987	706	19/35
1988	1149	10/20
1989	1403	--/21
Total	5707	700/ 191

Source: South African TRC, 1998, vol. 2, p. 389

The civil war also negatively impacted the family and social life as it contributed to family violence, disruptions of traditional and social cultures, invasion of homes, separation of family members and inter family conflicts in the community (South African TRC, 1998). Prolonged detentions also resulted in the breakdown of marital relationships due to their inability to function in expected family and social roles (Rupp & Sorel, 1998). This caused family disintegration, poverty and the degradation of living conditions (Engdahl & Fairbank, 1998; HRC, 1990). An unmeasured cost included the value of time contributed by family members to caring for their sick family members as many had to leave their job or business which added further stress on the family (South African TRC, 1998,, vol. 5, ch.4, p. 154). Economic hardship disrupted 51% of people's relationships due to the loss of income. Further, this cost was not confined to one generation as it hampered future generations through disrupted schooling and a lower ability to earn (South African TRC, 1998, vol. 2, ch.4, p. 154).

The South African Truth and Reconciliation Commission

The repression that underpinned life in South Africa during apartheid is well known, as is the resistance to it (Monama, 1996 cited in Stanley, E, 2011). From racial oppression, to torture, massacre and economic deprivation, the violence suffered by the masses was upheld on economic, political and judicial terms (Davis, 1991). The TRC, established under Nelson Mandela's government on 19 July 1995, heralded the most ambitious and organised attempt to deal with crimes of a past regime through a concept of truth (Amnesty, 1992; Wilson, 1995).

Background of the Establishment

After nearly 20 years of civil war, the political delegates met in Johannesburg under the auspices of convening a democratic South Africa (Thompson, 1995). Although this meeting failed, it led to a series of secret meetings that facilitated a return to the negotiating table (South African TRC, 1998). The participating parties agreed on an interim constitution in November 1993 with democratic elections to be held in April 1994. In recognition that political change would not be enough to heal the damage caused by decades of political struggle (Interim constitution, Ch. 16, 1993), the South African TRC was established to seek truthfulness from all participants in the South African conflict and offer amnesty with respect to crimes that might have been committed (DeRouen & Heo, 2007).

The National Unity and Reconciliation Act (the Act 1995) charged the TRC with i) investigating and documenting as complete a picture as possible of gross human rights violations committed within or outside South Africa in the period 1960 to 1994 and ii) to fairly and fully report the motives and perspectives of both the alleged perpetrators of gross human rights violations and of their victims. This was a difficult, challenging but necessary task to promote reconciliation and the reconstruction of a new democratic society that valued national unity and hoped to establish a more peaceful future (Stanley, 2001).

The Objectives/ Role of TRC in South Africa

The South African TRC was conceived as part of the bridge-building process designed to help lead the nation away from a deeply divided past to a future founded on the recognition of human rights and democracy. In other words, the telling of the truth about past gross human rights violations, as viewed from different perspectives, sought to facilitate the process of understanding divided pasts, whilst publicly acknowledging previously "untold suffering and injustice" (South African TRC, 1998, vol. 1, ch. 4, p.48). It also sought to help restore the dignity of victims and afford perpetrators the opportunity to come to terms with their own past (South African TRC, 1998; Preucel & Mrozowski, 2010).

The South African TRC had four major tasks to achieve to help promote national unity and reconciliation (South African TRC Act, 1995, Sec 14). The first task was to analyse and describe the causes, nature and extent of gross violations of human rights that occurred between 1 March 1960 and 10 May 1994, including the identification of the individuals and organisations responsible for such violations. Second, it was to make recommendations of reparation and rehabilitation to the President on measures to prevent future violations of human rights. Third, it was to help restore the human and civil dignity of victims of gross human rights violations through testimony and through the recommendations to the President for reparations to victims. Fourth, it was to grant amnesty to persons who made full disclosure of relevant facts relating to acts associated with a political objective.

The Structure/ Composition of the TRC

South Africa was the first country to initiate sustained public involvement in the commissioner selection process (Graybill, 2002). Nominations were first solicited from civil society and nominees were interviewed by a selection panel which was itself multiracial and included representatives from major political parties, trade unions and civil society. After public interviews with almost 300 nominees, the selection panel created a shortlist of candidates. Of these, 25 names were presented to the President and cabinet. The President then requested that the public submit questions for the final interview, further increasing public participation and interest, before he selected the final 17 commissioners. The commissioners had various political backgrounds and included human rights activists, lawyers, theologians, historians, social workers and psychologists (Government Gazette No. 16885, 1995). To assist the TRC in meeting its objectives, the TRC Act established three sub-committees, the Committee on Human Rights Violations (HRV Committee), the Committee on Amnesty (Amnesty Committee) and the Committee on Reparation and Rehabilitation (R&R Committee). The TRC also had its own investigative unit and witness protection program (South African TRC, 1998).

Table 7.4: Structure of the South African TRC

Main Committee	Different Committees	Different Units
TRC Committee -17 members	1. Human Rights Violations Committee - 8 members	1. Investigation Unit- support to Human Rights Violations and Amnesty Committees
	2. Amnesty Committee - 3 members	2. Department of Justice- assists in establishing office and infrastructure of TRC
	3. Reparation and Rehabilitation Committee - 5 members	

Source: Migyirka, 2008; South African TRC, 1998

Findings and Recommendations of South African TRC

The findings and recommendations of South African TRC are presented below.

Findings of the South African TRC

The TRC of South Africa presented its final report to the President on 29 October 1998 (South African TRC, 1998). It found the major causes of conflict in South Africa stemmed from the country's long-term socio-political situation which the TRC described in four parts, the Cold War, the anti-colonial/ decolonization context, the apartheid context and the racism context. The international climate of Cold War was a foundational cause of the civil war in South Africa, contributing to the particularly virulent form of anti-Communism and anti-Marxism that took root in South Africa after the 1948 election victory of the NP. The anti-Communist zeal of the Cold

War was an important factor in shaping the South African government's actions in the 1960s. This was exacerbated by South Africa's diplomatic alienation with Britain and the Commonwealth in the early 1960s as the notion of a common struggle against Communism and its forces was popular among key policymakers in the country. In this, the adoption of the Freedom Charter in 1955, the relationship between the ANC and the South African Communist Party (SACP) after 1960, and the ANC's later links to China and then the Soviet bloc entrenched the ruling government's perceptions of Communism and the struggle against white domination. The TRC found that South African society became largely divided into two opposing and rival groups, Communists and Marxists. As such, all opposing parties were labelled as Communist due to the global Cold War environment between 1960 and 1994. Likewise, any black opposition was considered illegitimate, and those associated with such opposition were criminalised. This was another factor contributing to the start of the civil war in South Africa (South African TRC, 1998, vol. 2).

The second wider context that contributed to the civil war was the anti-colonial resistance movement in Africa, particularly in the neighbouring territories of Zimbabwe, Namibia, Angola and Mozambique. This occurred over the same period and became deeply entangled with the South African struggle. Although the liberation movement was dominated by the non-racialism (maintain the vision of racial equality) of the ANC and anti-racism of other movements such as Black Consciousness, some organisations interpreted it as a struggle against whites. The tide of decolonisation that swept through Africa served only to reinforce the tendency of whites to regard blacks as the enemy (South African TRC, 1998).

The third and most direct political context was the NP policy of apartheid, long rooted in colonialism and segregation that was increasingly prevalent from 1948, particularly after the banning of the Pan Africanist Congress (PAC) and the ANC in 1960. This caused direct struggles between the oppressed and the oppressors that intensified into armed conflict over subsequent years. The apartheid system was maintained through repressive means, depriving the majority of South Africans of the most basic human rights, including civil, political, social and economic rights. Its legacy was a society in which vast numbers of people suffered from pervasive poverty and lack of opportunities and this drove the people to protest against the government (South African TRC, 1998).

The fourth key reason for long-term conflict in South Africa was entrenched racism. As an ideology, racism was a means of domination and oppression, providing the central grounds for the systematic exclusion, segregation and denigration of the black majority. Due to racism, progress in South Africa was by 'separate development'; any developments for blacks were slower as they were regarded as essentially different from the 'white' people. Politicians, leading academics, scientists, theologians and churches such as the Dutch Reformed Church (DRC) provided constant fuel to bolster such ideological positions. This served to distance and dehumanise the black population and opened the way for violence (South African TRC, 1998).

The discrimination and differentiation of black to white people fuelled apartheid. For example, the policy of consistent racial separation introduced in 1910 curtailed the rights of the black majority (Kumarasamy, 2012). The 'Mines and Works Act' of 1911 limited black workers exclusively to manual work with better positions going to white workers (Stewart, 2012). The 'Native Land Act' of 1913 set aside 7.3% of South African territory as reservations for black people and barred them from buying land outside these areas (ibid). Marriage or any love relationship between members of different racial groups was forbidden, and in all public institutions and offices, in public transport and public toilets, racial segregation was enforced. More detrimental however was the apartheid education system. The so-called Bantu education did not encourage black children to learn formal subjects and instead included dish washing and weeding of flowerbeds. Deprived of the right to vote or to strike, the black population had no political influence. Hence, the African National Congress (ANC), and other resistance and liberation movements emerged (ibid).

The TRC (1998) named the state and its security forces as the primary perpetrators of gross violations of human rights in South Africa between 1960 and 1994. In these unlawful activities, the state acted with certain political groups such as the Inkatha Freedom Party (IFP). The secondary largest perpetrators were allies of the state. For example, members of the State Security Council (SSC), including former President P. W. Botha, were responsible for unlawful activities such as killing political opponents and gross abuses of human rights. Their militant rhetoric created an acceptable climate where violations of human rights were possible. The TRC thus found them guilty of official tolerance of violations and accountable for such violations.

The former Government and its official bodies like the cabinet of the government, the National Intelligence Service (NIS), the security branch of the South African Police (SAP) and the SADF (South African Defence Force) perpetrated different human rights violations (South African TRC, 1998, p. 223). They also deliberately and systematically destroyed state and official documentation, in particular, valuable documentation of extra-parliamentary opposition to apartheid over a number of years. The mass destruction of records impacted on South Africa's social memory and also severely hampered the work of the TRC to promote reconciliation and healing through a disclosure of the past (South African TRC, 1998, vol.5, ch.6, pg 226).

Finally, the TRC found other elements in society acted as allies of the state in carrying out human rights abuses. These groups included Homeland Security Forces, Inkatha Freedom Party, Right-wing opposition groups, the Third Force, ANC, PAC, United democratic Front (UDF), and civil society (health sector, faith communities, business sector, media, and judiciary) (South African TRC, 1998).

Recommendations of the South African TRC

The South African TRC worked for seven years to fulfil its objectives of finding the truth of gross human rights violations and recommending measures to establish peace. It made different recommendations for peace through reparation, rehabilitation, reconciliation, and changes in rules and regulations (South African TRC, 1998, vol. 5, ch.8). Primarily, it recommended an ongoing commitment to reconciliation and unity, healing, reparation and rehabilitation to help prevent gross human rights violations in the future and promote organizational management.

The TRC requested the President to call a National Summit on Reconciliation as a part of its recommendations (South African TRC, 1998, vol. 5, p. 304). To prevent a repetition of the past, the TRC recommended the government close the gap between the advantaged and disadvantaged in society, create job opportunities, prioritize economic justice against poverty and take all possible measures to overcome racism (South African TRC, 1998, vol. 5, ch. 8, p. 308). To complete the reconciliation and peace process, the TRC recommended that prosecution be considered for perpetrators where evidence existed and when amnesty was not sought or denied (South African TRC, 1998, vol 5, p. 309).

To promote healing and rehabilitation, the TRC recommended the government fully utilize the services of non-government organizations (NGOs) to establish clinical and other appropriate services to facilitate the rehabilitation of perpetrators. Similarly, it recommended reparations of financial support of US$3,500 each year, for six years, to each victim or family. Further, the TRC recommended the government to address the rule of law, human rights practice, transparency, accountability and to root out corruption and other forms of criminality at all levels of society. To further advance this, the TRC recommended other sectors such as prisons educate prisoners and officers about human rights and for faith communities to promote reconciliation by developing appropriate theologies (South African TRC, 1998, vol.5, pp. 309, 313, 315, 316).

The TRC recommended the establishment of a business reconciliation fund as well as the creation and reservation of jobs and skill training, especially for victims. Resource generating programs such as compensation with land, as well as providing banking services to the victims, aimed to promote economic development and reduce the gap between rich and poor. The Commission further recommended the government and business sectors to facilitate economic development, industrial growth and agricultural expansion (South African TRC, 1998, vol. 5, pp. 319-321).

The TRC emphasized the importance of the justice system in aiding the establishment of peace. Hence, it recommended access to justice for victims of crime by establishing a serious crimes compensation fund, as exists in countries like Australia, if feasible. They also recommended access to justice for accused persons, and training and education to administer justice, the protection of witnesses and complainants. The reformation of different aspects of society such as the security forces, armed forces and the health sector was also necessary to protect against gross human rights violations. The controls on the media were also reduced so that it could play a role in uncovering and exposing evidence of gross violations of human rights (South African TRC, 1998, vol. 5, pp. 322-332, 334, 341).

Lastly, the TRC recommended the government of South Africa ratify the international covenant on civil and political rights, archive the works of the TRC, and prevent records of the country being destroyed, however unpleasant. The TRC recommended and urged that the President of the Republic of South Africa, as the Head of State, apologise to all victims on behalf of perpetrators from the security forces of the former state, and armed forces of the liberation movements, who committed gross violations of human rights (South African TRC, 1998, vol.5, pp. 337, 343, 345, 348).

The South African TRC: Strengths and Limitations

South Africa experienced 34 years of apartheid so the TRC had a broad area to cover to help establish peace in the country. Basically, the TRC was established to find the truth of gross violations of human rights, including the whereabouts of victims and identifying those responsible for human rights abuses, either directly or indirectly. Similarly, it was established to recommend steps to reform the institutions, provide reparation to the victims for the harm they had suffered and punish perpetrators. In these regards, the TRC of South Africa was successful.

The South African TRC also succeeded in educating the South African population about its functions and procedures. The South African Broadcast Corporation aired special reports on the TRC every Sunday from April 1996 until March 1998, and the program often scored amongst the most popular on South African television (Gibson, 2006). Hence, the TRC was successful in getting the attention of the people, persuading them of its views of the struggle over apartheid and collecting the truth on the conflict. Due largely to this, the TRC process was persuasive and succeeded, in part due, to the nature of the truth it promulgated (Gibson, 2006). Although there were limited available means, the TRC was also successful in uncovering past atrocities (Theissen, 1999) and establishing that gross human rights violations were committed (Dyzenhaus, 2000, p. 483). The TRC had a clear vision to address the economic causes of the civil war so another area of success was to provide the ways to reduce the economic differences between the poor and rich such as the creation of job opportunities, prioritization of economic justice against poverty, and taking all possible measures to overcome racism through a business reconciliation fund (TRC, 1998, vol. 5, p. 308).

Further, the commission was successful in identifying historical causes that intensified the conflict in the country. As the commission acknowledged, the system of rule established during the apartheid era was one of the main causes of civil war in the country. For example, whites were granted access to the rule of law but black citizens were not; 'Giving victims an opportunity to tell their stories is [also] a form of recognition that acknowledges the historical fact of their exclusion from legal recognition ... [and] is related to justice ... because it acknowledges the injustice of the exclusions that made [it possible for] abuses [to occur]' (Dyzenhaus, 2000, p. 484).

The most important success of the South African TRC was, as Beer and Fouche (2000) analyzed, publishing a report criticized by all sides of the political divide. Former President F W de Klerk managed to remove some of the most damaging findings about him. Similarly, the ANC tried to stop the release of the report because it was strongly criticized for human rights abuses and for violations committed by Winnie Mandela, the ANC women's league leader, and her football club.

However, there were some limitations in the functions of the TRC. These included insufficient time to collect the information through hearings and insufficient finances. The TRC therefore failed to deal with significant geopolitical areas, and the violations that occurred in those areas, in sufficient detail. For example, the violations primarily perpetrated by security force members in areas such as Venda, Lebowa were not reported in sufficient detail. Hence, thousands of victims could not share their experiences with the commission. As a result, the TRC did not record a full account of South African life under apartheid (Stanley, 2001).

Further, despite offering amnesty in exchange for perpetrators' detailed stories and threatening prosecution for those who remained silent, the majority of perpetrators did not come forward (Stanley, 2001). Although the TRC promised reparation assistance, not many victims come forward to record their truth. Thus, the social and criminal justice that underpinned the TRC philosophy, such as prosecuting and punishing perpetrators, was not realised. For example, the perpetrators of violence, and beneficiaries of apartheid, have had no obligation to make any substantive changes, and neither the TRC nor the government have sufficiently challenged the structural inequalities which contextualised apartheid policies (Zehr, 1997).

The TRC also failed in its objective of balancing other problems such as crime, violence, and unresolved land issues. The reticence to settle reparations has led some to comment that the Commission was flawed in its focus, particularly as 'perpetrators' were granted immediate freedom with amnesty, while victims continued to wait to be financially acknowledged (Ash 1997; Sooka, 2003). The commission did not make clear which victims deserved reparations and what they would consist of (Verdoolaege & Kerstens, 2004). As the TRC was not successful in all areas of its recommendations, many areas and 'communities' in South Africa remain dislocated and characterised by poverty, lack of good housing, poor education, limited health services and unemployment (Stanley, 2001). Whilst the Commission successfully provided a forum for diverse expression, acknowledging personal suffering and the promoting a more truthful future it has also left South Africa ultimately unsatisfied (Rosenburg, 1999, p. xi).

Table 7.5: Strengths and Limitations of South African TRC

Strengths		
S.N.	**Causes of war which was addressed**	**Recommendations**
1	Gap between the advantaged and disadvantaged	Rule of law, human rights practice
2	Poverty	Prioritize economic justice
3	Racism	Rule of law, human rights practice
4	Corruption	Rule of law, human rights practice, transparency, accountability
5	Economy (gap between rich and poor)	A business reconciliation fund, creation and reservation of jobs, skill trainings, resource generating program, industrial growth, agricultural expansion
6	Human rights violations	Rules and regulations, human rights practice, reformation of security forces, armed forces and health sector, apology by President
7	All the root causes	Reconciliation, rehabilitation, reparation, a serious crimes compensation fund
8	Rehabilitation and healing	Full utilization of NGOs; clinic and appropriate services

9	Reparation	Financial support for six years

Limitations/ weaknesses

S.N.	Weaknesses	Reasons
1	Lack of full truth	Short of time and budget
2	Less perpetrators came forward	Threatening prosecution who remained silent
3	Less victims came forward	Lack of making to understand prosecuting and punishing the perpetrators
3	Lack of coverage of all the areas	Lack of focus on all areas
4	Lengthy reparation to victims	Immediate focus on perpetrators

Source: South African TRC, 1998

Conclusion

In conclusion, the TRC of South Africa was successful in covering most of the areas of the causes and consequences of the civil war (South African TRC, 1998, p. 306). These included the anti-colonial, apartheid and racism contexts as well as the wider Cold War atmosphere. Further, it was successful in promoting the peace process by recommending the government address poverty, racism, corruption, and the human rights violations through revised rules and regulations, and its good practices. However, the South African TRC was unsuccessful in finding the full truth as it could not cover all the areas of the country due to insufficient budget and time. Thus it made inadequate recommendations in all sectors and was ultimately unsuccessful in achieving its aims to promote social and criminal justice and reconciliation.

CHAPTER 8

Comparative Analysis of the Case Studies: Liberia, Sierra Leone and South Africa TRCs

The case studies of the TRCs in Liberia, Sierra Leone, and South Africa provide useful insights into the actions, recommendations, strengths and limitations of the functions of the commissions in those countries. This chapter compares the TRCs of these three countries with Nepal's TRC. As discussed in Chapter 3 and 9, even though the TRC was established in Nepal in 2015, it has not been a smooth process due to different factors. Hence, this comparison of the functioning of other TRCs aims to identify factors and methods to help the Nepali TRC move forward and act to address, and reconcile, the causes of the country's civil war and its consequences.

Comparisons on TRC

The countries of Liberia, Sierra Leone, South Africa and Nepal each experienced civil war. The signing of a peace agreement in these countries opened the way to establish a TRC to promote peace and reconciliation. However, the background of the establishment of each TRC, their functions and recommendations were different in each case.

In the case of Liberia, the CPA took place in August 2003 after 15 years of civil war. This cleared the way to establish a TRC. The Head of the National Transitional Government of Liberia, Charles Gyude Bryant, constituted a nine member TRC on 4 January 2004. Unfortunately, it failed to gain legitimacy; it then took another two years for the President of Liberia, Ellen Johnson Sirleaf to officially establish Liberia's TRC on 20 February 2006. It was launched with a two year mandate, up to September 2008, but was extended by 10 months until 30 June 2009 (Liberian TRC,

2009). This commission also comprised nine Liberian commissioners. An International Technical Advisory Committee (ITAC) representing the Economic Community of West African States (ECOWAS) was also established in 2006 by the United Nations High Commissioner of Human Rights (UNHCHR). The ECOWAS representatives resigned within a short time so in September 2008 the UNHCHR and ITAC nominated other members who were appointed by the President in July 2008 (Liberian TRC, 2009).

In Sierra Leone, the peace agreement between the Government of Sierra Leone and the RUF- party was signed on 7 July 1999. Although this agreement mandated the establishment of a TRC within 90 days, it was not established until November 2002 and ran until October 2004 (USIP, 2002). The commission consisted of seven commissioners, four Sierra Leoneans and three internationals from Gambia, Canada and South Africa respectively (four men and three women), three executive secretaries, 216 staff members, 21 consultants, and 14 interns. The members were nominated and appointed by President Kabbah (Liberian TRC, 2009).

The South African TRC was established in 1995 after the abolition of apartheid in 1990. It was mandated to operate between 1995 and 1998 but was extended until 2002 thus it worked for seven years to help promote reconciliation and establish peace in South Africa. The commissioner selection process in South Africa was unique because nominees were first solicited from civil society. A selection panel that included representatives from all major political parties, trade unions and civil society interviewed the resulting 300 nominees to determine 25 potential commissioners. Thereafter, a final interview decided the 17 commissioners who were appointed by the President (Graybill, 2002). The 17 commissioners (nine men and eight women) were from different backgrounds including politics, human rights, law, theology, history, social work and psychology. The commissioners were supported by nearly 300 staffs and three different committees - the Human Right Violations Committee, the Amnesty Committee and the Reparation and Rehabilitation Committee (Migyirka, 2008).

Table 8.1: Comparisons of TRCs in Liberia, Sierra Leone, and South Africa

Area	Liberia	Sierra Leone	S. Africa
Time taken to establish TRC after Peace agreement	3 years	3 years	5 years
Duration of TRC	2 years but extended by 10 months	2 years	3 years but extended in total to 7 years
Number of Commissioners	9 commissioners	7 commissioners, 3 executive secretary, 216 staff, 21 consultants, 14 interns	17 commissioners with 300 staff
Nationality of Commissioners	Liberian	4 Sierra Leonean, 1 Gambian, 1 Canadian, 1 South African	South African
Number of committees	Advisory committee of 3 members	None	3 committees

Source: TRC, 1998, 2004, 2009

Comparisons on TRC Findings

The TRC findings are described in causes and consequences of war as-

Causes of War

Each TRC collected information regarding the causes and effects of the civil war in the respective country, the number and types of gross human rights violations committed, and the situations of perpetrators, the victims and their families/relatives.

The TRC in Liberia named corruption, poverty, limited access to education, and inequalities in economic, social, civil and political sectors in the country as the causes of the conflict. The greed of individuals exacerbated corruption in every sector in Liberia and the unequal distribution of land further contributed to the conflict between settler and indigenous Liberians. The social and legal systems played a vital role in polarizing these two groups of people and were ultimately further causes of the civil war. External factors, such as the role played by the USA, also contributed to the civil war in Liberia (Liberian TRC, 2009, Vol. II).

The TRC of Sierra Leone found the major causes of the conflict included the failure of leaders to run the government, nepotism and greed, such as the plundering of gold and diamonds that promoted corruption and increased poverty in the country. The lack of positive and progressive policies, and policies that favoured particular ethnic groups and discriminated against others (Richards, 2003) were further causes of conflict in Sierra Leone, as was the loss of hope among the youth due to the non-accountability of the government and its bodies. The active role played by Charles Taylor was another major factor in starting, and extending, the civil war in Sierra Leone (Sierra Leonean TRC, 2004).

The South African TRC worked for a long time to examine and review events that occurred during the 34 years of apartheid. Apartheid policies in South Africa were a major cause of the long civil war. Racial separation was introduced to segregate blacks and whites in 1910, in 1913 the Native Land Act barred blacks from buying land outside the South African territory (BBC, 2013), marriage between black and white was forbidden, racial segregation was enforced in all areas of life and the low standards of enforced education for blacks all contributed to the conflict in South Africa. The anti-colonial resistance movement in the neighbouring countries of Zimbabwe, Namibia, and Angola was another motivator among the South African people to fight against apartheid between 1960 and 1994 (South African TRC, 1998).

Consequences of War

All the warring parties in each country were responsible for domestic and international war crimes and human rights violations. Killing, abduction, assault, and looting and enforced displacement were common consequences of the civil wars.

Major consequence of the war in Liberia were the death of 250,000 people and displacement of 1.5 million people, the exploitation of forests and diamond mines and large scale damage to the physical structures of the country (Liberian TRC, 2009, vol. 2).

In Sierra Leone, the human rights violations included mutilation, murder, child labour, sex labour, rape, abductions, arbitrary detentions, looting, torture and forced displacement. External actors, including Libya, Liberia, Charles Taylor and the National Patriotic Front of Liberia (NPFL), United Movement for Democracy (ULIMO), Economic Community of West Africans States (ECOWAS), and Economic Community of West African States Monitoring Group (ECOMOG) were also responsible for the civil war and human rights violations in Sierra Leone (Sierra Leonean TRC, 2004).

In South Africa, under apartheid, many people, predominantly black, suffered rape, sexual assault, beating, torture, abduction, shootings, burnings, poisoning, mutilation, destruction of houses, and separation from family members that often caused psychological effects, loss of independence and dignity. South Africa, unlike other countries, experienced the killing of people by burning and neck lacing (see Chapter 7) (South African TRC, 1998).

Table 8.2: Comparisons on findings by TRC in Liberia, Sierra Leone, and South Africa

Findings	Liberia	Sierra Leone	S. Africa
Causes	Poverty, limited access to education, inequalities in economic, social, civil and political sectors Greed, corruption Unequal land distribution Social and legal system Historical causes Role of USA	Failure of leadership in the Government Greed, corruption, nepotism Unaccountable Government towards the public and civil society Colonial strategies of divide and rule Death penalty and misuse of emergency powers	The Cold War Anti-colonialism and segregation Racism Former Government and President and some political parties/ groups' corruption

Violations/ Effects	Human rights violations, gender based violations, 250,000 were killed, 1.5 million displaced, corruption, destruction of economic sectors such as forests and diamond mines, destruction of physical structures	Human rights violations, displacement of 2 million from birth place, abductions, amputation, arbitrary detentions, killing of 50,000, forced recruitment and sex slavery of children	Human rights violations abduction, severe ill treatment (sexual assault/ abuse, rape or harassment, destruction of homes, mutilation of body parts, necklace murder) Internally displaced, and disappearance
Warring Parties	Violator groups – 10 Lesser violator groups – 11 Military institutions- 2	Internal actors – 10 External actors – 5	Different groups - 8+ Different Government sectors- 2

Source: TRC, 1998, 2004, 2009

Comparisons on TRC Recommendations

The TRC recommendations are compared in the areas as general, reconciliation, reparation and other areas.

General

The TRCs of the three countries made recommendations to promote peace, reconciliation and reparation in different ways.

The Liberian TRC made recommendations to the Head of State and to the Government. The recommendations focused on reparation, rehabilitation of victims and perpetrators, legal and institutional reforms, amnesty, and prosecution of offenders in a special court (Liberian TRC, 2009).

The major recommendations of the Sierra Leonean TRC focused on building a new and democratic Sierra Leone. In reconstructing the country, the recommendations prioritised health and education and emphasised the reparation process, equal opportunity, and abolishing discrimination against women by establishing the rule of laws, improving governance and prosecuting corruption to uphold human rights with equal respects to all (Sierra Leonean TRC, 2004).

In the case of South Africa, the TRC recommended the Government to address the causes of the conflict as well as focus on reconciliation and reparation procedures. The recommendations included making a national commitment to the promotion of reconciliation and unity, the prevention of gross human rights violations in the future, and processes for accountability, healing and rehabilitation, organization, administration and management. The archiving of the commission's materials and public access, as well as preservation of documents, were other recommendations in the South African TRC's final report (South African TRC, 1998).

Table 8.3: Comparisons on general recommendations by TRC in Liberia, Sierra Leone, and S. Africa

Liberia	Sierra Leone	S. Africa
Recommendations to the Head of State: Reparation and rehabilitation for both victims and perpetrators, legal reforms, continue investigation, prosecutions in particular cases **Major Recommendation to the Government and all:** Extraordinary criminal court, domestic criminal prosecutions, public sanctions, National 'Palava Hut' program, economic crime investigation, reparations, good governance, and others	Human rights protection, establishment of rule of law, security services, good governance, focus on youth, women and children, reconciliation, reparation, archiving TRC documents, follow up committee	Human rights protection, reconciliation, prosecution, rehabilitation, reparation, good governance, different culture promoted in sectors like prison, faith communities, business, legal, security forces, health sector, media, archiving TRC documents

Source: TRC, 1998, 2004, 2009

Reconciliation

Reconciliation is the process of coming to terms with past acts and enemies; this includes finding a way to live that permits a vision of the future and the rebuilding of relationships to promote a society-wide, long-term process of deep and broad change while acknowledging, remembering and learning from the past to enable a better future (Bloomfield et al, 2003). National reconciliation thus plays a vital role in establishing peace and promoting the long-term process of healing. As Bloomfield et al (2003) describe, reconciliation can be achieved in a variety of ways such as forms of retributive or restorative justice, historical accounting of events via truth-telling, and reparation for the material and psychological damage inflicted on the victims. Restorative justice can thus help the processes of healing and rebuilding. In addition, telling the truth also facilitates reparation and reconciliation (Torpey, 2003; Walker, 2010).

Reconciliation largely depends upon the commitment of the country's Government, political parties, victims, perpetrators and population in general. The President, as the chief of the country, can actively encourage reconciliation by ensuring the broadest representation from all sectors of the country and ask for full participation in the reconciliation process. To further promote the success of reconciliation, a strong human rights culture should be maintained. Hence, decreasing the gap between advantaged and disadvantaged groups in the community is important and can be facilitated by providing job opportunities through economic development.

To reconcile victims, as well as perpetrators within the same community, wounds inflicted as a result of the conflict should be healed. This can be promoted by encouraging all parties to tell the truth about human rights violations, with the Government then officially acknowledging the crimes and apologizing to the victims. Decriminalization, exoneration, exhumation and reburial are other avenues to promote reconciliation.

In the case of Liberia, the TRC recommended a special 'Palava Hut' program be instituted to provide opportunities for people to tell the truth about their past experiences. The program aimed to allow rural communities to resolve conflict and begin the reconciliation process. The TRC also recommended 45 people be prosecuted for economic crimes and that all assets acquired unlawfully during the conflict be seized (Liberian TRC, 2009).

The Sierra Leonean TRC focused on promoting reconciliation in several ways. These included having all the actors involved in the Civil War apologize and performing symbolic activities such as establishing monuments on mass graves and commemorating an annual National Day on 18th of January involving victims, ex-combatants and other members of communities in traditional, religious, social, recreational and sports activities to further promote the reconciliation process. To promote equal opportunity within society, the commission recommended the quota system in political parties. For example, 30 percent of seats would be preserved and separated for women and 10 percent for the youth, especially during the political elections (Sierra Leonean TRC, 2004).

The South African TRC recommended restructuring some public sectors to help develop a culture of respect and promote reconciliation and peace. The TRC also recommended government agencies such as prison officers should be trained in human rights (South African TRC, 1998, vol.5, p.316) and for faith communities to advocate a forgiveness theology to promote reconciliation (p.316). The South African TRC advised the President, as the head of the state, to apologize to all victims on behalf of those perpetrators from the members of security forces of the former state and those armed forces of the liberation movements who committed gross violations of human rights (pp.347, 348).

Table 8.4: Comparisons on reconciliation process in Liberia, Sierra Leone, and South Africa

Liberia	Sierra Leone	South Africa
Public apology by the Government	Public apologies by all actors involved in the war	Public apology and official acknowledgement by the President
New political culture as anti-corruption, decentralization of power	Government and civil society engage on political, moral and social issue dialogues of the past, present and future	Decriminalization

Resourcing civil society for national building	Different activities between victims, ex-combatants and other community members such as traditional, religious, social, recreational and sports	Exoneration Exhumation and reburial Forgiveness
Equal economic, social and cultural rights to everyone	Equal opportunity in politics through quota system	Trainings to change attitudes in some governmental and non-governmental organisations to develop the culture of respect

Source: TRC, 1998, 2004, 2009

Reparation

Reparation plays a vital role in promoting the healing of war wounds. The TRCs in Liberia (2009), Sierra Leone (2004) and South Africa (1998) recommended different reparation processes.

In Liberia, a reparation Trust Fund of US $500 million was recommended to compensate victims. Free education at primary, secondary and tertiary levels of education was another recommended avenue of reparation. The establishment of community development projects for schools, health facilities, and roads - especially in the most victimized communities, empowerment programs for women including education and micro economic programs, psychosocial, physical, therapeutic, counselling, medical, mental health and other health related services were also part of the reparation processes. As an ongoing symbol of reparation, the Liberian TRC recommended memorial sites be built and a National Unification Day be recognised as a national holiday. Significantly, the Liberian Government issued a public apology which was an important aspect in promoting reparation in Liberia. The Liberian commission was the first commission that recommended the inclusion of the Diasporas to help in the reparation process by donating at least US$ 1.00 per month. The donation would go to the Reparation Trust which would be utilised in social engineering to rebuild public infrastructures.

The Sierra Leonean TRC recommended the distribution of service packages and symbolic measures to help meet the needs of victims. Significantly, it did not recommend cash payments to victims as part of the reparation process. The services included health initiatives– particularly in medical and psychological care, pensions, education, skills training and micro credit paid for through the Special War Fund for victims (Article XXIX Peace Agreement; Section 7(6) TRC Act). The health care program included free medical treatment, free healthcare to amputees, and free mental healthcare treatment. The provision of free education until senior secondary level, and skill training programs for victims, were other important aspects of the reparation program to promote the rebuilding of the country. The community reparation was prescribed to rebuild the infrastructure and included the building of a national war memorial as a symbol of remembrance and reparation in Sierra Leone (TRC, 2004, p.196).

In South Africa, the reparation program would help victims and the country move forward. The South African TRC proposed a US$3,500 payment each year for six years to victims and/or their family through the President's fund as financial reparation. The money was a symbol of a commitment to reparation, as was the issuing of death certificates, the erection of monuments and memorials and proclaiming a National Day of Remembrance. Renaming streets and public facilities were further acts of symbolic reparation in South Africa. Importantly, the TRC of South Africa recommended the Government fully utilize the cooperation and capabilities of Non-Government organizations (NGOs) establishing clinics and providing the appropriate services to facilitate the rehabilitation of perpetrators (vol.5, p. 309). In the sector of community reparations, the Government launched community based services and activities including a demilitarization program for youth, mental health services, counselling, community colleges and youth centres, basic education and training for adults, skill based employment training for youth, housing projects, and laws to prevent human rights abuses in the future.

Table 8.5: Comparisons on reparation process in Liberia, Sierra Leone, and S. Africa

Reparation	Liberia	Sierra Leone	S. Africa
Financial	US$500 million to victims over 30 years through trust	No financial help	US$ 3500 each year for six years to victims
Symbolic	A National Day	A National war memorial	A National Day
		Building infrastructure in the most affected areas	Erection of monuments and memorials
			Renaming street and public facilities
			Issuing death certificates
Community	Physical, psychological, therapeutic. Counselling, medical, mental and other health services	Pension for adults as the amount determined by NACSA monthly	Community based services such as demilitarization programs for youth
	Community development projects	Free education and skill training to victims	Free community colleges and youth centres
	Education and small business		Basic education and training for adults
			Housing projects
			Laws for human rights
Diaspora and international community	Donation of at least US$ 1.00 per month to reparation trust fund		
	Help from UN, foreign states, INGOs, donors		NGOs for perpetrators

Source: TRC, 1998 2004, 2009

Other areas

Each TRC made recommendations on other areas to the country's Government.

The Liberian TRC covered different sectors widely in its recommendations. It recommended the extraordinary criminal court address the gross human rights violations such as the international humanitarian law and human rights law, war crimes, economic crimes, killing, gang rape, multiple rape, forced recruitment, sexual slavery, forced labour, exposure to deprivation, and missing persons (Liberian TRC, 2009). It strongly recommended people who committed violations during the period of 1979-2003 not to be able to hold any appointment for 30 years from 1st of July 2009 and the prosecution of 116 persons, including Charles Taylor. The Liberian TRC also recommended building a new political culture, resourcing civil society for nation building, providing equal economic, social and cultural rights to everyone, protecting children, resourcing an independent human rights commission, the decentralization of political and economical power, and poverty reduction.

The Sierra Leonean TRC recognised that without the presence of good governance, the country could not achieve any of its goals. Hence, the Sierra Leonean commission recommended the Anti-corruption Commission to promote and equip public servants to follow and uphold the Code of Ethics in their service to the Nation. The Commission recommended establishing a human rights commission to protect and uphold human rights in the country. It recommended covering these fundamental rights in the constitution as well as abolishing the death penalty and gender-based discrimination. Importantly, the TRC recommended the local courts and public defence systems protect human rights (Sierra Leonean TRC, 2004). Other recommendations to address the human rights protection were the establishment of a compensation fund, reformation of the security forces and health sectors and more press freedom to report incidents (Sierra Leonean TRC, 2004, vol.5, pp. 322-341).

Similarly, the South African TRC recommended the rule of law, transparency and accountability be strengthened to uproot corruption and better protect human rights (South African TRC, 1998, vol.5, p. 313), including access to justice for crime victims, protection of witnesses and complainants (pp. 322-328). Reformation in education, as well as training army, security force and police officers to protect human rights were further recommendations (pp. 328-332). The provision of health facilities to all war victims, and greater freedom to the media to report the war and its impacts, including the human rights abuses so everyone could understand the causes, impacts and ratifying procedures to balance the human rights were further recommendations of the TRC (pp. 334-341). The TRC of South Africa also recommended providing banking services to generate resources as well as develop an environment for economic development so that the gap between poor and rich would be reduced (pp. 319-321).

All the TRCs recognised the need to guard against a repetition of the human rights abuses and conflicts they had experienced. The Liberian TRC recommended an encyclopaedia of Liberian culture and history be prepared to help educate future generations. Both the Sierra Leonean and South African TRCs recommended preservation of all the documents, videos and audio tapes, pictures, photographs, and database information from the TRC so people could see and better understand the effects of civil war and human rights violations on a country (Sierra Leonean TRC, 2004, pp. 313, 343, 345). Similarly, as a post peace process, the Sierra Leonean TRC suggested the establishment of follow-up committee to monitor the activities towards the peace process (Recommendation tables; vol 2, pp. 206-225).

Table 8.6: Comparisons on other processes in Liberia, Sierra Leone, and S. Africa

Others	Liberia	Sierra Leone	South Africa
Human rights preservation	Extraordinary criminal court, restriction to appoint violators for 30 years, prosecution	Human rights commission, fundamental rights in constitution, compensation fund, reformation in security forces and health sectors, freedom to media	Rule of law, transparency, accountability, access to justice, reformation in education as well as training of Code of Ethics, role of media

Further development of peace	New political culture, resourcing civil society, equal rights of economic, social and cultural, protection of children, Resourcing independent human rights commission and anti-corruption commission, decentralization of political and economic power, poverty reduction.	Good governance, anti-corruption commission, new principles of national security	Banking services, economic developments
Protection from repetition of conflict	Encyclopaedia of Liberian culture and history	Preservation of TRC records such as documents, videos and audio tapes, pictures and photographs, database, follow-up committee	Preservation of TRC records such as documents, videos and audio tapes, pictures and photographs, database

Source: TRC, 1998, 2004, 2009

CHAPTER 9

The TRC of Nepal and its Functions

The Nepali Truth and Reconciliation Commission

The Comprehensive Peace Agreement (CPA) mandated the Government of Nepal establish a Truth and Reconciliation Commission (TRC) in 2006. The TRC in Nepal was to be established to promote the processes of peace and reconciliation between the warring parties (CPA, 2006). However, it has taken nine years to establish the TRC in Nepal. In this time, multiple factors have delayed its establishment, as observed by the Government and concerned political actors (The Kathmandu Post, 2015). These factors include the instability of the Government, a lack of will from major political parties to establish the commission and international politics are and examined in this chapter. The Nepali TRC was finally established in February 2015 (Kantipur, 2015) however little progress has been achieved to date (TRC Interim Report, 2016). This chapter builds on Chapter 3; while it provided the background for establishing a TRC in Nepal, this chapter explores the implementation and progress of the Nepali TRC.

The Objectives/Mandates of the TRC in Nepal

The Nepali TRC's mandate by the National Assembly is defined in the Investigation on Enforced Disappeared Persons (IEDP) and TRC Act 2014. In brief, the TRC in Nepal has six major tasks to achieve (TRC, 2015); it is to investigate and publish incidents of gross human rights violations committed between 13 February 1996 and 21 November 2006. It is to identify the victims and perpetrators of civil war in Nepal and promote reconciliation between them. It is to recommend compensation for the victims and their families as part of the reparation process to help compensate, in part, for the violations endured during the civil war. It is to identity victims to officially record the events and inform the reparation process. And it is to make recommendations to the Government for legal action against the perpetrators if amnesty will not be granted, and in the cases where reconciliation cannot be reached. The TRC recognised that implementing these objectives will be difficult and divides the mandate into three different sections; a mandate of functions, duties and powers of the commission, a mandate on investigations, and a mandate on recommendations.

The mandate for the functions, duties and powers of the TRC has the power to investigate incidents of gross violations of human rights and consult and investigate incidents with the concerned court and authority. The TRC can determine if cases took place during the conflict or not. To ensure the TRC can complete its procedures, especially the collection of information, the TRC can make separate arrangements for victims filing a complaint to be heard by the Commission (TRC Act, 2014). The TRC mandate on investigations has a wide range of powers including ensuring informants' and victims' security, searching a person's place and belongings without notification if the commission thinks it necessary and suspending a person from their workplace if there is a risk he/she will destroy evidence from his/her office. The TRC mandate on recommendations details the steps toward promoting reconciliation, reparation, rehabilitation and returning property to the victims and recommends actions to provide justice for victims and perpetrators.

The Reconciliation Commission has the mandate to promote mutual reconciliation when/if perpetrator/s and victim/s makes an application to do so. During the mutual reconciliation, the commission may cause the perpetrator to apologize and offer reasonable compensation to the victim. It can further promote reconciliation by organizing reconciliation functions at the sites of conflict; constructing statues and monuments in public places; publishing articles and literary works concerning reconciliation; and by enhancing social and communal good faith by carrying out other appropriate acts. In instances where a victim was a minor or has died, the commission has the mandate to bring about reconciliation between the perpetrator and the family of the victim.

In the case of reparation, the commission will make recommendations to the Nepali Government to compensate the victim/s via restitution, rehabilitation or other appropriate arrangements. It can recommend the Government provide facilities to the victim or any member of his/her family including free education and medical treatment, skill oriented training, loan facilities without interest, arrangements for settlement, employment and other facilities or concessions as the commission deems appropriate. In the case of returning property, the commission can recommend property be returned if it was captured or seized. The commission can also recommend reasonable compensation to the victim for his/her actual loss of the captured/seized property.

In the case of recommended actions, the commission can recommend the Government take proper action against any person who was involved in the offence of gross violations of human rights during the civil war. In the case of amnesty, the commission can recommend the Government grant amnesty to any perpetrator on the basis of conditions and criteria, as referred to in IEDP and TRC Act 2014 (Section 25, Sub-section 4, 5 and 6). However, the Act (Article 2J) does not grant blanket amnesty in the cases of punitive human rights violations or abuses in extrajudicial killings, enforced disappearances and rape cases (IEDP & TRC Act, 2014; Pathak, 2015). The commission may recommend amnesty to those perpetrators who submit an application within the time frame specified by the commission, mentioning the truth and facts on the activities carried out in the armed conflict and expressing regret for their acts during the civil war while promising not to repeat any such act in the future. However, if the commission makes a recommendation for amnesty the perpetrator may need to provide reasonable compensation to the victim for the loss he/she suffered.

Table 9.1: Objectives/mandates of the TRC in Nepal

Investigate and publish the incidents/realities of gross violations of human rights violations	Investigate the realities of gross violations of human rights
Recommend processes to promote reconciliation	Recommend processes to promote the reparation processes
Recommend the rehabilitation and return of property to victims	Amnesty (rare) to the perpetrators with conditions

Source: Nepali TRC, 2015

The Structure/Composition of the Nepali TRC

A TRC was constituted by the Government of Nepal, Council of Ministers on 10 February, 2015 in accordance with the IEDP and TRC Act, 2014. A five-member committee, headed by former Supreme Court Chief Justice Om Bhakta Shrestha was established on 16 June 2014. It worked for eight months to finalize a list of officials and presented their recommendations to the Prime Minister, Sushil Koirala and the Government of Nepal established the TRC on 10 February, 2015 (The Rising Nepal, 2015).

Eight sub committees were established to be responsible for different tasks.

Table 9.2: Structure of the TRC in Nepal

Truth and Reconciliation Commission of Nepal (with its sub-committees)	
1.Procedures relating to conduct of business of meeting draft sub-committee	2.Code of conduct drafting sub-committee
3.Format development sub-committee	4.Rules drafting sub-committee
5.Dialogue, consultation and communication sub-committee	6.Structure of commission development team
7.Victim, children, senior citizens, persons with disability and women friendly structure sub-committee	8.Financial rules sub-committee

Source: Nepali TRC, 2015

Delayed Establishment

A number of political factors that threatened law and order also paralyzed the establishment of the TRC in Nepal. While all political parties understood the peace process as a power-sharing agreement between them, the major elements of the peace process were reduced to bargaining chips in the struggle for immediate benefits of power-sharing and longer-term re-alignments between, and within, the different parties (International Crisis Group (ICG), 2011). Hence, each party was more interested in establishing a monopoly of power sharing than establishing the TRC. As a result, both democracy and promoting the peace process through the TRC become casualties of shifting political powers (Bhatta, 2012).

The lack of political understanding and consensus among the political parties, on the fundamental processes that govern how a TRC stands and works, further delayed its establishment (Tamang, 2012). From 2011 to 2013, Nepal suffered political deadlocks because the political parties could not reach an agreement to appoint an interim election council (IEC) headed by a non political Prime Minister. This was largely because the different parties could not agree among themselves on a political coalition to govern and were more concerned with their own interests and benefits (Asian Network for Free Election (ANFREL), 2013). This prolonged political wrangling contributed to unstable conditions for Government, as evidenced by the appointment of eight Prime Ministers within 10 years from 2006, and further delayed the formation of the TRC as it was supposed to be established under broad political understandings and based on consensus among the political parties (Tamang, 2013). Hence, the establishment of the TRC was permanently overshadowed by these political actions, as detailed below.

The factions of political parties in Nepal have also delayed the formation TRC as the political parties are engaged in the formation of new parties. Overall, the major parties such as the Nepali Congress fractioned into Nepali Congress, Madheshi Janadhikar Forum (MJF), Madheshi Janadhikar Forum Madhesh (MJFM) and Tarai-Madhesh Loktantric Party (TMLP). Factions in the Maoist Party resulted of five different parties such as Communist Party of Nepal-Maoist or CPN (M), Janatantric Mukti Morcha (JTMM), Communist Party of Nepal-Maoist (CPN-M), Communist Party of Nepal Maoist (CONM) and New Force Party (NFP).

During the CA election in 2008, under the proportional representation system, each party had to present their own closed lists of candidates which left the room to favour the nomination own relatives in CA i.e.; the parties had promoted family friendly politics. As a result, the 28 families, made up of husband and wife teams, represented in the Constitution Assembly (CA). Their political power and involvement in corrupt practices delayed the establishment of the TRC in Nepal. Combined with the rise of armed non-state actors in the southern flatlands of Nepal bordering India and the eastern hills from groups including the Madhesi Mukti Tigers, United Janatantrik Terai Mukti Morcha, Terai Cobra, and Janatantrik Terai Mukti Morcha-Rajan, the political dynamics in Nepal further hampered the establishment of the TRC (Bhatta, 2012).

The involvement of international forces in Nepal's peace and constitution building process was another critical factor in delaying the establishment of the Nepali TRC. India's involvement in encouraging the Madhesi political parties from the Southern Terai plain of Nepal, for example the protest against the demand called for the 'liberation' of the entire Terai by redrawing the region into a single autonomous unit called Madhes, unsettled the then Maoist Government (Miklian, 2008). This was because the then Nepali Prime Minister visited China in 2008 (BBC, 2008) instead of India. This China visit contributed to deepening tensions between India and the UCPN (Maoist Party). This resulted in the dissolution of the Constitutional Assembly (CA) from 2006 to 2014 (Tamang, 2011).

The Nepali TRC was finally established on 10 February 2015 to examine human rights violations during the conflict and create a forum for social reconciliation (Kantipur, 2015).

Table 9.3: Delayed establishment of the TRC in Nepal

Interim constitution	Could not work out as it was interim
TRC Bill	Inadequate consultation with civil society,
	insufficient guarantees of independence from the government and political parties,
	limited mandate, absence of recognition for the rights of victims and witnesses
Politics	Unstable Government due to political shifts, absence of seriousness,
	power plays and power sharing,
	International interventions (India)

Source: Bhatta, 2012; Gonzalez, 2012; ICG, 2011; ICTJ, 2011; TRC, 2016;

Factors impacting the slow Functioning of the Nepali TRC

Just as the Nepali TRC was slow in being established, its functioning is equally slow moving. Different factors are responsible for this sluggishness, including the political situation in Nepal, the lack of established acts, rules and regulations, the Maoist party, insufficient manpower and budgets, a devastating earthquake, and the influence and interests of international stakeholders. Among these factors, the political scenario has been one of the most challenging. Instead of focusing on restoring peace, the political parties have focused on strengthening their positions to form their own majority Government. This has delayed and slowed the TRC's functioning. The Nepali TRC and the Commission of Investigation on Enforced Disappeared Persons (CIEDP), for example, recommended the Government bring in a law to criminalise torture. These bodies also sought amendments in the TRC Act to define some crimes, and to over-rule the statute on the limitation for rape, especially for the incidents of rape that were committed during the decade-long People's War (Maoist insurgency). However, to date, the Government has not acted on either (ICTJ, 2016). The TRC did not have working regulations until 14 months after its establishment, nor did it have a budget. Six months after its formation in mid 2015, the commission forwarded draft regulations to the Government of Nepal, but the Government did not endorse them until 19 March 2016 (Rai, 2016).

The main party in the civil war, the Maoist party, voiced concerns over provisions in the draft regulations, saying it was a political war and any incidents could not be judged by a civil court but through a political consensus; problematically, this process does not consider the victim (Bastola, 2012). Similarly, the Maoist party delayed the progress of the TRC by strongly condemning the provisions relating to i) issuing arrest warrants against perpetrators, ii) invalidating their passports and iii) the courts handing down verdicts in conflict-era cases. The provisions in the draft that made it mandatory to seek the victims' consent for pardons, even after the courts ordered a pardon for the perpetrators, was also objected to by the Maoist party (My Republica, 2016). These delays have also made it more difficult to find evidence of crimes, thus complicating the steps of uncovering the truth on human rights violations (Jha, 2015).

Even though the TRC had been formed, 14 months have passed without any significant progress in its functions due to a lack of TRC regulations. To implement and uphold justice for Nepali victims, different laws should be in place, for example, a Witness Protection Act, Transitional Punishment Act, Crime Humanitarian Law, and a Retroactive Law. However, all of these laws are so far, absent in Nepal. The vagueness of the power relationships between the court and the TRC is also delaying the functioning of the TRC. For instance, the TRC has been provided with powers by the TRC Act 2014 to demand papers from the court with regard to cases that have been filed and investigated. It is not clear however if the court's investigation will be stopped once the TRC begins its examinations. This has led to a kind of parallel jurisdiction, which potentially creates problems and has a direct impact the functioning of the TRC (The Kathmandu Post, 2015).

The universal jurisdiction in criminal law for cases of human rights abuses requires the Government of Nepal to provide working regulations for the smooth functioning of the TRC. This law enables human rights abusers from any country to be arrested in any other country. Colonel Kumar Lama of the Nepal Army was arrested in Britain in January 2013. His charges were based on allegations that in 2005, during Nepal's decade-long internal armed conflict (People's War) between the Government and Maoist forces, Colonel Lama participated in the torture of two detainees at an army barracks under his command (BBC, 2013). Despite these allegations, the coalition Government failed to provide the necessary regulations to the TRC until 14 months after its establishment, thus immunizing themselves from this international law. Similarly, the Government has not amended the laws for amnesty to serious crimes such as torture and the act of disappearance even after 23 months of the Supreme Court order to do so (Kantipur, 2016).

Other factors have further slowed the progress of the Nepali TRC. Within 14 months of its formation, the TRC was reeling under budget constraints as less than half the amount of the required funds had been released. While the TRC requested NRs 140 million, the Government had released NRs 90 million only. The shortfall in the budget directly affected the functions of the TRC. With not enough funds and a lack of regulations, the commission has not been able to work smoothly or progress its work (Kathmandu Post, 2016).

Unfulfilled promises from the top leaders are also the cause of slow functioning of the TRC. For example; according to NHRC; Pushpa Kamal Dahal (The Moist Supreme Commander) promised to help the TRC when he was the Prime Minister of Nepal between 18 Aug 2008 and 25 May 2009, and between 4 Aug 2016 and 31 May 2017. He promised to resolve all outstanding issues of the peace process, but he neither amended the TRC Act nor released budget for TRC to appoint adequate staff (The Himalaya Times, 2016).There is inadequate resources of human, financial and technical which are major obstacles of the TRC for its smooth performance effectively and efficiently (ICJ, 2017).

There has also been a significant increase in the influence of other countries on Nepali politics since the insurgency and the palace coup in 2005 (Bhatta, 2013), especially from India (Muni, 2012). The Indian Government now provides scholarships to the children of political leaders, including the Maoists, as well as children of high profile bureaucrats and civil society elites, irrespective of their competency; this is concerning as these individuals may then act to support India's interests in Nepal rather than representing the Nepali people. Seemingly, the peace process in Nepal is of little interest to the major political parties and leaders unless it is beneficial to India. Arguably, given the Comprehensive Peace Accord 2006 (CPA) was completed in Delhi, India, this is not surprising (Bhatta, 2013). The lack of cooperation from political parties and their leaders in Nepal is one of the major issues hindering the work and progress of the Nepali TRC.

Similarly, until and after the promulgation of a new constitution for Nepal, the Government has been delaying solving the issue of state restructuring, as raised by the Madhesi political forces. This question became problematic when India supported protesters and imposed an unofficial blockade on Nepal that has been in place since September 2015 (BBC, 2015). Because of this, the Nepali Government has had to divert its attention and resources to resolving this problem, further hampering the functioning of the TRC.

At present, the parties involved in the peace process are unwilling to negotiate. The parties can be divided into two groups: those who support the Government and those who oppose it. The opposing side includes the Madhesi political parties, Tharus (Kantipur, 2016) and although a comprehensive outline to guide and enact the peace-making processes is required, these factors are impeding the functions of the TRC.

In April 2015, Nepal experienced a major earthquake that extensively damaged the countryside and infrastructure of the country. The earthquake again diverted the interest of the political parties away from the peace making process. Moreover, the centralized management of relief materials enabled a systemic practice of corruption to develop. Security forces, members of the bureaucracy and members of political parties were found to be openly involved in this corruption yet the Government failed to take any action (Elliot, 2015).

Table 9.4: Factors contributing to the slow functioning of the Nepali TRC

Factors	Situation
Political situation of the country	Parties focused on making Government and not on promoting the peace and reconciliation process
Lack of working acts, rules and regulations	Absence of Witness Protection Act, Transitional Punishment Act, Crime Humanitarian Law, Retroactive Law, no working regulations until 14 months after its establishment
Concerns of the Maoist party	Concerns on judgement by the court, arrest warrants against the perpetrators, invalidation of their passports, victims' consent for pardons,
Insufficient manpower and budget	TRC requested NRs 140 million but the Government released NRs 90 million only
Devastating earthquake	Earthquake diverted the interest of political parties, socio-economic turmoil since 25 April 2015
International interest	India

Source: BBC, 2015; Bhatta, 2013; Elliot, 2015; Himalayan Times, 2016; ICTJ, 2016; Jha, 2015; Kantipur, 2016; Kathmandu Post, 2015; MyRepublica, 2016

Progress to date

The Nepali TRC and CIEDP have warned the Government many times of the dangers of delay in addressing the serious crimes and human rights violations that occurred during the decade-long People's War (Kantipur, 2015). Despite the extensive delays it has experienced, the Nepali TRC prepared and submitted interim reports to the President of Nepal on 7 Feb 2016, one year after the formation of the commissions (The Himalayan Times, 2016). The report was detailed; it comprehensively identified the work, challenges and future plans of the TRC and offers the conclusions drawn from the commissioners' interactions with conflict victims, civil society and journalists from 52 districts across the country (TRC-Nepal, 2016).

The report contains different sections, including the duties and responsibilities of the TRC, the functions it has accomplished from 10 Feb 2015 to 6 Feb 2016, suggestions regarding the functions of the TRC from stakeholders, challenges experienced and facing the TRC, future plans and recommendations to support the TRC in its functioning. While it is expected the commission will deliver victim-centric justice, such outcomes remain undecided because of the absence of regulations, the lack of support from the Government and the stalemate in negotiations between the different political parties (Kantipur, 2015).

One year after the establishment of the TRC, the interaction programs on the activities of the Nepali TRC, with representatives from Government, civil society and journalists, and conflict victims have been established in 20 out of 75 districts in Nepal, and separately conducted by office bearers of the Commission. From these interaction programs, the TRC collected suggestions from the victims and their family members, civil society, journalists and others (Interim Report, TRC-Nepal, 2016).

The suggestions mainly focused on providing temporary relief measures such as medicine for the victims and their families. Other suggestions focused on the criteria to categorize the victims because of the rise in claims by 'fake victims' through different political parties. Further suggestions to the TRC from the victims and their families included scholarships to the children of victims, ongoing health treatment for victims as they still face health issues, life skills training, employment opportunities, help to orphans and cash help for the victims to the value of NRs. 100,000 per person.

To help meet these suggestions, the TRC requested the Government provide a sufficient budget, manpower and facilities and implement related regulations; skill based training and effective help to support its functioning. It demanded the complete amendment of TRC Act 2014 and lawful criteria to categorize real victims so false victims would be punished. Further, it suggested increasing the budget by NRs. 1.5 million for health treatment to the victims, as well as providing a cash amount of NRs. 100,000 to every victim as temporary support. Psychological treatment, scholarships to the children of victims, protection of orphans, protection of property of victims, and a one door system to provide help for unlawfully detained victims as soon as possible were some of the other recommendations included in the interim report of the Nepali TRC.

After submitting the interim report, the TRC still awaited the decision of cabinet for its regulations so that it could effectively function. Due to the lengthy delay in reaching a decision, the chairman of the Nepali TRC warned the Government that the United Nations (UN) was already skeptical of Nepal's ability to effectively manage a transitional justice system. He added that it would be unfortunate for Nepal and Nepalis, as well as Nepal's independence, if Nepal's judicial system failed to deliver and it would be taken as an invitation for foreign intervention, including from the UN (The Himalayan Times, 7 Feb 2016).

International practice is that if a Government cannot support the TRC to resolve human rights violations that occurred during an insurgency, the international community, such as the UN, would establish a tribunal and prosecute those involved in serious crimes (Pandey, 2017). Furthermore, if the TRC failed to work, as per international standards in the absence of suitable regulations for it, the international community would not accept Nepal's decisions and could demand mechanisms of international justice, akin to events in Sri Lanka where the Government of Sri Lanka was totally disregarded. This was because they were unable to establish and apply the rule of law and international standards so an international mechanism to prosecute those responsible for mass human rights violations was demanded and created (Khatiwoda, 2016, Kantipur, 2016, MyRepublica, 2016, Amnesty International, 2012; Human Rights Watch, 2013; Clarke, 2011).

Considering the potential for such an event to occur in Nepal, on 18 March 2016, the Government of Nepal endorsed the regulations of the Nepali TRC (The Kathmandu Post, 2016). The Nepali TRC received its regulations just 10 months before its allocated time duration to complete the task. However, the TRC Act 2014 allows the commission to expand its functions for one further year. The TRC published its schedule, including the expanded one year time duration to complete its tasks and achieve its objectives (TRC, 2015).

In real time, the Nepali TRC has spent one year trying to make progress; it has not begun to address the need to develop a legal framework, or the real task of documenting and investigating cases of human rights abuses (Kantipur, 16 Feb 2015). The TRC is yet to recruit and train employees for its purposes (Kathmandu post, 2016). The TRC also now doubts the neutrality of the existing peace committees, which are basically all-party mechanisms; it therefore plans to set up a separate mechanism in all districts to collect complaints from conflict victims. This is because many fake victims received relief as the district based Peace Committees failed to work properly (Nepalekhabar, 2016). As it is not possible to collect the complaints by immediately establishing local offices, the TRC has decided to collect complaints through the existing local Peace Committees as the best option in a short time, and given the lack of budget and manpower (Kantipur, 16 Feb 2015). Hence, the TRC gave public notice on 17 April 2016 those complaints of human rights violations that took place during the People's War in Nepal were to be lodged within two months (TRC, 2016). It provided options for the complainants' to submit claims either to the head office of the TRC in Kathmandu, the capital city of Nepal, or with one of the 75 local Peace Committees (TRC, 2016). The TRC will accept complaints about human rights abuse cases such as killing/murdering, abduction or taking hostage, mutilation or disability, physical or mental torture, rape or sexual abuse, looting or the destroying of properties, and any acts against the international human rights and laws. Up to the last of December 2016, the Nepali TRC had received 58,052 applications (TRC, 2016). Given the response, on the 20th of July 2016, the Government of Nepal decided to increase the time duration of existing local Peace Committees by one year to better support the work of the TRC (The Kathmandu Post, 2016). Similarly, the TRC extended the date for victims to lodge complaints until 10 August, 2016.

The two-year term of the TRC of Nepal expired without it completing its tasks on 8 February 2017. The Government of Nepal extended its tenure by one year on 9 February 2017 as per Clause 38 (2) of the TRC Act 2014 which allows the Government to do this if necessary (Republica, 2017).

Table 9.5: Progress of the TRC in Nepal to date

Interim reports on 7 Feb 2016 to the Government of Nepal	Interaction programs on the activities of the Truth and Reconciliation Commission with the representatives of Government officials and offices, civil society and journalists, and conflict victims

Recommendation for the TRC regulations and endorsed on 18 March 2016	Published work plan
Public notice 17 April 2016 to apply for complaints of human rights violations	Acceptance of complaints until 18 July 2016 extended until 10 August 2016

Source: Kantipur, 2015; Nepalekhabar, 2016; The Kathmandu Post, 2016; The Himalayan Times, 2016; TRC, 2016

Criticisms to Nepali TRC

A TRC is established to find out the truth and provide justice to the victims as well as perpetrators so that they can live together in the same community with dignity. If the Commission works independently and without prejudice, it will be possible to make perpetrators accountable and provide redress to victims. However, more than two years after the commission was established, these functions have largely remained unfulfilled (ICJ, 2017) because its functioning has been stalled due to different reasons. This has provoked individuals, institutions, civil society organizations and victims to criticize it. The absence of political will is a major factor impeding the commission's function. For example, even though the Supreme Court declared in February 2015 that amnesty cannot be granted for serious crimes like rape, forced disappearances, extrajudicial killing and torture (Global press journal, 15 Aug 2016), the two major political parties i.e.; the Communist Party of Nepal-Unified Marxist Leninist (CPN-UML) and the Maoist (now is Maoist Center) signed a nine-point agreement on 5 May 2016 which contains provisions for general amnesty to perpetrators. As the Attorney General Raman Kumar Shrestha opposed the recommendation that no general or blanket amnesty (Kathmandu Post, 2016), the commission's recommendation and the Supreme Court's ruling was ignored.

The absence of political will within Nepal's ruling Government to bring perpetrators to justice is the major obstacle to addressing violations and abuses committed during the People's War. This lack of will has impeded the pace and the dynamic of the transitional justice process in Nepal (ICJ, 2017). The Human Rights Activist, Mandira Sharma, has criticized the Government's failure to address the ongoing issues from the People's War and the surviving families and their associations feel the transition to peace is guided by political, rather than humanitarian or moral concerns (Bhandari, 2015). Due to the delay, serious discussion has occurred about the best ways to address the past atrocities. Similar to the ruling Government, the security apparatus has not wanted the Nepali TRC to succeed (BBC, 2016).

Different organizations have also criticized the lack of action of the Nepali TRC. However, due to the lack of international obligations in the TRC Act, the UN is unabile to support the TRC in the prevailing circumstances (Accord, 2017). Thus, the TRC is essentially toothless because it lacks any enforcement mechanisms (Open society Foundation, 2016). As a result, the international donors and human rights organisations have kept their distance from the work of the TRC and CIDP (Mandira Sharma, Accord, March 2017, London).

Like the UN, the National Human Rights Commission (NHRC) has raised concerns about the lack of the TRC to achieve its basic duty to resolve human rights abuses during the People's War. The Chairman, Anup Raj Sharma, is particularly concerned about the TRC's approach of not consulting conflict-victims to investigate complaints and criticized the growing hostility among TRC members (Himalaya Times, 2016).

The coordination and victim-friendly mechanisms between the TRC and other organisations is also ineffective. Due to this, the documenting of a large number of human rights violations and abuses during the People's War has not been shared with human rights organizations leaving the TRC's records incomplete. The lack of confidentiality in the resolution of human rights abuses process is a further criticism and raises concerns about security threats to those who engaged with the TRC and registered complaints (ICJ, 2017).

The entire reconciliation effort has been plagued with problems. For example, the selection of members was political and lacked transparency. The selection was carried out without any consultation with victims and human rights groups (ICJ, 2017). The appointment of five-member commissioners was manipulated by major party leaders with the intention to influence the investigation of the cases in their favour (Global Press, 2016). Although the commissioners belong to advocates, civil servants and academics from different backgrounds, there is an absence of civil society representatives despite this representation being imperative for the TRC to implement one of its key recommendations (Himalaya Times, 2017). The functioning of the TRC has been further stalled by internal feuding between the members as well as alleged partisan interests from different political parties (Republica, 2016). The rifts between the commissioners who represent contrasting political ideologies are thus leading the TRC nowhere (Kantipur, 2017).

Mistrust in the intent of the Nepali TRC is rising. The failure of the Supreme Court of Nepal to establish international standards on transitional justice or jurisprudence means the TRC is unable to adopt a victim-friendly approach to its mandate (ICJ, 2017). As a result, there is no role for victims in the truth and reconciliation process. Unless a deeper victim-centred justice process is articulated, the TRC process will not be able to address the core needs of victims (Bhandari, 2015).

A culture of impunity has a priority in Nepal and within Nepali politics. For instance, victims or rape and torture have a 35-day statute of limitations to register cases. Despite immense pressure from civil society, the Government and TRC have not yet developed and enforced the required laws and policies to address this problem (Open Society Foundation, 2016).

The prolonged delay in the delivery of truth and justice is angering the victims. In November 2016, a group of former Maoist combatants picked and padlocked the Maoists' office with a demand for compensation for the exploitation as child soldiers. In February 2017, hundreds of victims' families protested in front of the Parliament Secretariat in Singha Durbar, Kathmandu demanding justice. And more recently, on 28 August 2017, the families of police and army personnel who fought against the Maoists during the People's War also protested in front of the TRC office, Kathmandu. The delay in the Nepali TRC delivering justice is now sowing the seeds for future conflict instead of promoting reconciliation and recovery (The Himalayan Times, 2017).

The slow and frustrating progress of the Nepali TRC makes victims doubt they will receive justice. This is because of the actors of People's War i.e.; the Maoists and other political parties are running the Government in syndicate way (power sharing mechanism) so there is a possibility to sideline the truth and justice by them (Kantipur, 4 April 2017).

Table 9.6: Criticisms to Nepali TRC

Lingering on amnesty matter.	Lack of will among major political parties.
Lack of enforcement mechanisms.	Lack of consultation with victims.
Presence of de jure and de facto impunity, weak centralized institutions and weak rule of law.	Lack of confidentiality and security for the victims who engaged with the TRC.
Lack of transparency during the selection of the TRC members which was a political motivation.	Lack of international standards.
Presence of a culture of impunity.	Presence of doubt as the powerful actors of People's War holds the key power of the Government.

(Source: Bhandari, 2015; Himalayan Times, 2017; ICJ, 2017; Kantipur, 2017)

CHAPTER-10

Conclusion and Recommendations

Summary

This book has focused on the role of the Truth and Reconciliation Commission (TRC) in Nepal's peace process. It has reviewed the background causes of the conflict in Nepal, from 1995 to 2005, and the consequences of this conflict that need to be addressed in the peace process. The TRC, as an institution, has a vital role in establishing, facilitating and managing the peace process by addressing and recommending to the Government how to reconcile the country considering the causes and consequences of the war and progress into the future. In this regard, the thesis examined, analysed and compared the case studies on the role and successes of previous TRCs in South Africa, Liberia and Sierra Leone to help inform and promote progress in finalizing Nepal's peace process.

Key Findings

This book was concerned to examine two study questions. First, the background of the conflict in Nepal and the key impacts of the conflict. Second, the role of the TRC in facilitating and establishing peace in Nepal. The findings on these two questions are summarised below.

What were the causes of conflict in Nepal?

Nepal has experienced an interwoven and complex web of socioeconomic, legal and politico-ideological problems for many years. Thus, in Nepal, socio-cultural, political and individual factors were the major causes of the war. They included the inequitable socioeconomic situations of the majority of the population, the entrenched discrimination against the poorest Nepalis (Karki & Bhattarai, 2003; Hachchethu, 2005, Venhaus,

2010), the feudal social structure, the indifference to oppressed ethnic groups (Katsiaficas, 2013), the structural poverty (Hutt, 2004; Joshi & mason, 2007; Lawoti & Pahari, 2009), the caste system (Mahat, 2005), discrimination against women (GoN, 2011), and the Hinduist suppression of peoples' culture and religion (Shakya, 2006).

Nepal is a multi-dimensional country in terms of culture, ethnicity, religions and language. It has 125 dialects and 61 ethnic groups, with Hinduism and the Nepali language dominating since the unification of the Nepalese kingdom 235 years ago (Gurung et al, 2000). This has resulted in Hinduism and Hindus being considered as the upper class in Nepal and this divided Nepali society into two parts i.e. upper class and lower class including the so-called untouchables, the Dalits. The long-term oppression, neglect, and refusal to address social and economic inequalities, as well as failing structural factors, energised the oppressed ethnic and lower class groups to take part in the insurgency. All these issues frustrated many people, predominantly those from the rural areas of Nepal. The Maoists, identifying these problems, put forward new ideas of social justice. These new ideas played on individuals' consciousness to support the insurgency that began in 1995.

The ongoing corruption, lack of stability and bad governance made the people seek radical options. The Government excluded many minorities, indigenous, ethnics and marginalized populations from the parliamentary representation so they were not represented in the policy and decision-making processes in Government. As the people did not feel part of the democratic process they were ready to participate in the civil war (People's War) to help deliver institutionalized bureaucracy, more balanced representation, and stable Government. Lack of personal fulfilment due to poverty, mistreatment and discrimination such as torture by the authorities and the desire to feel safe prompted many people to join the insurgency, thinking they would receive all the basic needs after winning the war.

What were the major societal impacts of the conflict in Nepal?

Thousands of people were killed, disabled, and displaced during the insurgency, resulting in many people being orphaned, widowed and disappeared. Incidents of human rights were rive, and included torture and disappearances, as discussed in Chapter Two. Over the 10 years of turmoil, every sector of Nepali society suffered from the Maoist insurgency (People's War).

Physical infrastructures such as the drinking water and electricity systems, telecommunication system, suspension bridges, historical monuments, public buildings and institutions and personal property were severely damaged or lost. The economy generating sectors of Nepal such as agriculture, industry, employment, tourism, and foreign aid were acutely disrupted for an extended period because of the insurgency. As a result, Nepal's economic activities declined and this has contributed to the younger generations migrating overseas for employment opportunities.

How can the TRC play a role in Nepal's peace process?

A TRC is an institution that is instigated for peace management and to facilitate a larger program of justice, especially in a transitional or post-conflict situation. Hence, it is an important avenue to help deliver justice to both the victims and perpetrators of the human rights violations. In the case of Nepal, the Comprehensive Peace Accord (CPA) 2006 mandated the establishment of the Nepali TRC however due to different political circumstances the TRC was not established until 2015.

The TRC investigates the past and looks forward as it attempts to facilitate social transformation and develop a peaceful society for the future. It focuses on establishing democracy and establishing the rule of law by investigating, establishing and reporting the truth. The TRC achieves this by organizing hearings for victims and perpetrators to present their experiences, collecting evidence from various sources such as documents, newspapers and perhaps the strongest means - interviews. The final report the TRC prepares includes recommendations for rebuilding the divided society, mainly through the creation of an environment for sustainable peace and reconciliation, providing reparations to the victims and avenues of rehabilitation, as well as recommending any legal actions against persons who were involved in serious offenses against humanity. Most importantly, it recommends measures to prevent future human rights violations. The TRC is thus in a position of authority to facilitate the establishment of a social peace in Nepal.

How can case studies from other countries inform the role of the TRC in progressing and completing the peace process in Nepal?

As the TRC has practical truth-seeking functions to reconcile societies divided due to conflict, it can help reconcile a society's troubled past and address human rights violations for perpetrators and victims. Primarily, the TRC advocates justice to repair the past damage and heal the past human rights violations through different means such as financial help, different income generating training, health and education facilities, official apologies, commemorations, and the creation of a society where all people can live and work together.

In general, these three TRCs in Liberia, Sierra Leone and South Africa investigated the causes of the conflicts, the subsequent atrocities and consequences and then made recommendations to address these problems. Importantly, they focused on reconciliation, reparation, and rehabilitation to establish the peace and join the divided communities in their respective countries. Inherent in these processes was the ability of the TRC to address corruption, gender-based discrimination, health, education, press, security forces, prison, human rights abuses and rule of law. The studies of these different TRCs illustrate various pathways the TRC in Nepal may consider in progressing the peace processes as well as what to recommend to effectively address the problems brought by the war.

Recommendations

This book is concerned with progressing the peace process in Nepal. The most important measure for peace building is to redress the root causes of conflict. This is essential, as recognized by the President of the United Nations' Security Council (2001) in a Presidential Statement on peace building on 5 February 2001:

> The Security Council recognizes that peace building is aimed at preventing the outbreak, the recurrence or the continuation of armed conflict and therefore encompasses a wide range of political, development, humanitarian and human rights programs and mechanism. This requires short- and long-term actions tailored to address the particular needs of societies sliding into conflict or emerging from it. These actions should focus on fostering sustainable development, the eradication of poverty

and inequalities, transparent and accountable governance, the promotion of democracy, respect for human rights and the rule of law and the promotion of a culture of peace and nonviolence (pp. 1-2).

For the establishment of permanent peace, the negative, as well as positive peace should be established (Galtung, 1964, 1996). The negative peace is the absence of direct violence between individuals and groups through suitable mechanisms to avoid, reduce and manage conflict. On the other side, the positive peace is the integration of human society through social justice, equal opportunity, and rights under the laws of the country. Nepal has both negative and positive factors that need to be reconciled for the peace process. This thesis thus makes the following recommendations to facilitate the TRC establishing both negative and positive peace in Nepal.

The success of peace building is assessed by reviewing the likelihood of the recurrence of war and the quality of post-war governance (Doyle and Sambanis 2006). The recommendations to the TRC of Nepal focus on; first; the structure of the commission itself with its subcommittees and commissioners; second, implementing the recommendations to address the causes and consequences of the war to provide justice and facilitate the establishment of peace in the country through reconciliation, reparation, and rehabilitation procedures. The experiences of Liberia, Sierra Leone, and South Africa clearly illustrate how the workings of a TRC can address the causes and effects of the wars in their countries and promote peace.

Recommendations on Structure of the TRC

The signing of a peace agreement opened the way to establish a TRC in Liberia, Sierra Leone, and South Africa, however, each country nominated its commissioners differently. Sierra Leone and South Africa appointed several international commissioners who were human rights activists, lawyers, theologians, historians, social workers and psychologists (S. Africa Gazette No. 16885, 1995). The inclusion of international committee members could reduce bias and promote open-mindedness as opposed to local commissioners who may be influenced by political parties, local influences, and private concerns.

i. The commission should include national as well as international persons from different sectors such as human rights activists, lawyers, theologists, historians, social workers, psychologists and United Nations' representatives.

Recommendations on the Causes and consequences of civil war

Unless the causes of civil war in Nepal addressed, the peace process and the establishment of peace will not be completed. As the major causes of war were socio-cultural, political and individual, the TRC should recommend the Government, as well as related organizations, political parties and individuals (within the country and Diasporas), address these causes to help expedite the peace process.

Until the signs of the consequences brought by the Maoist war are erased, the people will not move past the war and its pain. Hence, the consequences are to be addressed to help the people reconcile themselves and feel peace in their community.

Recommendations on the socio-cultural causes of civil war

Multiple, long-term socio-cultural inequities in Nepali society contributed to the war.

i.   Nepal needs to maintain and protect human rights as well as social rights and uphold equal opportunity for everyone without any discrimination on caste, gender and ethnicity (Sierra Leonean TRC, 2004; South African TRC, 1998).

ii. Discrimination against women should be addressed by implementing quotas for women strictly, which is present in the New Constitution of Nepal, in the political parties in public elections so they can represent themselves.

iii. Resourcing civil society as well as providing the social and cultural rights to everyone, as in Liberia (TRC, 2009), to address the presence of discrimination between upper and lower class/caste as well as the oppression and suppression in Nepali society.

iv. Human Rights should be protected strongly through the Human Rights Commission of Nepal and should be included in the constitution of Nepal. Furthermore, social engineering is a major task for the Nepali Government to establish peace and equity in society.

Recommendations on Political causes of civil war

Nepal's future development depends on upon how effective its Government is. In Nepal, the governing political parties and their leaders prioritized their interests before the country and people. Political struggle was the major factor driving the People's War. Political strategies need to be adopted to end Government corruption, nepotism and cronyism to achieve political stability (Hachchethu, 2005), ensure the inclusion of minorities in political representation (Gersony, 2003; Gurung, 2005; Hutt, 2004; Leve, 2007; Parvati, 2003; Thapa, 2004), and end elite domination of the states (Deraniyagala, 2005).

i. A primary recommendation is the reconstruction of a new political order, as undertaken in Liberia (Liberian TRC, 2009).

ii. The political class should implement plans to build a new Nepal. Their responsibilities/ duties and obligations should include the administration of justice, combating corruption, institutionalizing good governance and reducing poverty.

iii. Establish an Anti-Corruption Commission in Nepal to end endemic corruption as in Sierra Leone. Furthermore, political leaders and parties publicly commit themselves to the principles and practice of good governance (Sierra Leonean TRC, 2004).

iv. Promote freedom of political expression to all (Sierra Leonean TRC, 2004), including the equality of political representation, without discrimination to promote a vibrant and healthy democracy and to end political oppression and suppression.

v. The Nepali Government uphold the rule of the rule which is transparent and accountable at all levels of the Government, politics and society as occurred in South Africa (TRC, 1998).

Recommendations on Individual causes of civil war

The People's War in Nepal impacted on the lives of most Nepalis. Many of the poorest Nepalis participated in the People's War believing it was the only way to change their circumstances.

i. The Government is to address the poverty, especially among the ethnic groups, so-called low caste people to provide full and equal recognition of their economic rights along with social and cultural identities to ensure these minorities have access to economic opportunities for personal and group benefits.

ii. The creation of job opportunities, decentralization of economic power to support the economy through loans and grants, as occurred in Liberia and South Africa (Liberian TRC, 2009; South African TRC, 1998).

iii. Provide financial and banking services to help support economic development and reduce the gap between poor and rich (South African TRC, 1998).

iv. Establish an anti-corruption commission, as occurred in Liberia and Sierra Leone (TRC, 2009, 2004) and strong accountability measures be put in place as they were in South Africa (South African TRC, 1998).

v. Create job opportunities to help overcome the gap between rich and poor and to assist victims of the civil war in establishing a business reconciliation fund, as in South Africa (South African TRC, 1998).

vi. Reforming the Land Act 2012 (B.S.) for balanced distribution of land to every Nepali (Department of Land Reform and Management, Nepal; 2016).

vii. The Dalits, are the most disadvantaged in the Nepali caste system. They have high illiteracy levels and are landless (Mahat, 2005). Hence, use and management of land, as well as other natural resources to assist the Dalits, should be reviewed as in Liberia (Liberian TRC, 2009).

viii. The Nepali Government to apply strongly the new constitution of Nepal 2015 on all forms of discrimination and oppression relating to class, ethnicity, religion. Language and gender including all forms of racial untouchability should be made punishable (Constitution of Nepal, 2015).

ix. The introduction of Human Rights in the curriculum in high school level formal education to address the issues of racism, gender discrimination, conflict resolution and the rights of children, as in South Africa (South African TRC, 1995).

x.   Investigate police violence, repression, and abuse. Establish an Extraordinary Criminal Court, as in Liberia, to prosecute key police and army officers for gross human rights violations (Liberian TRC Report, 2009).

Recommendations on Socio-cultural consequences

Acknowledging crimes committed during the insurgency and apologizing to the victims is essential in the reconciliation process. This occurred in both Sierra Leone and South Africa (Sierra Leonean TRC, 2004; South African TRC, 1998). In Liberia, the President issued a public apology (Liberian TRC, 2009). Different reconciliation methods must be recommended by the TRC of Nepal to the Government of Nepal to address the socio-cultural consequences. Healing of war wounds can be made through the reparation programs in Nepal, as recommended below.

i.   Establish monuments for symbolic reconciliation, the celebration of a reconciliation day as a national day in which different Nepali traditional, religious, social, and recreational and sports activities would occur, similar to the measures undertaken in Sierra Leone (Sierra Leonean TRC, 2004).

ii.   The restructuring of Government institutions by promoting a culture of respect to assist the reconciliation and peace process. Nepal can follow as in South Africa, the prison guards, the police, and army officers were trained to protect human rights (South African TRC, 1998) to secure the trust of the people.

iii. Establish a Reparation Trust Fund. The Trust could be funded by all Nepalis and the Nepalis Diaspora. Non-Government Organizations (NGOs) and International Non-Government Organizations (INGOs) continue their work in reparation programs to sustain the peace, following the South African model (South African TRC, 1998) in Nepal.

iv.   The Reparation Trust fund compensation for war victims; free education to their children; community development projects such as free health facilities and services (medical and psychological care); empowerment programs like micro-economic programs including skill trainings, agricultural trainings especially to the women, as in Liberia, and the construction of roads which can bring development in rural areas (Liberian TRC, 2009).

v. Symbolic reparation is recommended in the renaming of streets, public facilities, as in South Africa. Reconstruction of destroyed physical structures (South African TRC, 1998) such as police posts, schools, Government offices and the houses of the victims to provide infrastructure for internally and externally displaced people.

vi. Laws to prevent the repetition of human rights abuses.

vii. Education and training and employment for the People's War victimized youths and adults (South African TRC, 1998).

viii. Establish an Extraordinary Criminal Court to prosecute individuals for gross human rights violations of international humanitarian law and human rights law, war crimes, and economic crimes. Building a new political culture, resourcing civil and political society for nation building to address the present political culture such as power game, strikes (Liberian TRC, 2009).

ix. Establish and resource a National Human Rights Commission (NHRC) to proactively combat corruption, institutionalizing good governance, promoting economic empowerment and facilitating poverty reduction.

Recommendations on Physical consequences

Different infrastructures of Nepal were destroyed during the 10 year People's War. All infrastructures should be re-structured within a certain time frame but this may be possible only through a special program, such as implemented in Liberia and Sierra Leone.

Although Liberia, Sierra Leone and South Africa had the problem of landmines and Improvised Explosive Devices (IEDs) the TRCs in these countries made no recommendations to address the issue. This research recommends the following steps to address the issue in Nepal.

The United Nations Children's Fund (UNICEF) and the United Nations (UN) have supported the Mine Action Work Plan since 2007 in cooperation with the Ministry of Defence (MoD) and Ministry of Peace and Reconstruction (MoPR) Nepal. Different actions have raised awareness of the impact of landmines and the need to stop using them including the importance of fencing minefields, using warning signs and starting to clear landmines (Nepal National Mine Action Strategy, 2011). At the end of 2014, the Mine Action Program ended despite landmines and IEDs still being an issue in Nepal.

i. Establish a Reparation Trust Fund (Sierra Leonean TRC, 2004; Liberian TRC, 2009). The fund could be directed for re-building of bridges, schools, health facilities, roads and public office buildings.

ii. Establish a National Landmine Action Authority (NMAA) which runs a special search program to locate the landmines and IEDs and clear out or dispose of them to protect Nepalis (GICHD, 2015).

Recommendations on Political-economy consequences

The main economic sources of Nepal are agriculture and tourism. These areas support various industries and create job opportunities and employment. But the insurgency ruined these sectors in Nepal. The TRC should recommend the recommendations to the Government of Nepal, the Nepalis Diasporas and the international community/donors as in Liberia (Liberian TRC, 2009).

i. The Government, Nepali Diaspora and international community/ donors relating to constructing a new Nepal through economic development by economic empowerment and poverty reduction.

ii. Establishment of new programs in the agriculture and tourism sectors.

iii. Establish a business reconciliation fund as well as the creation and reservation of jobs and skill training, especially for victims.

iv. Resource generating programs such as compensation with land, as well as providing banking services to the victims to promote economic development and help reduce the gap between rich and poor.

v. Government and business sectors facilitate economic development, industrial growth and agricultural expansion (S. African TRC, 1995).

vi.   The Nepali Diaspora should contribute at least US $30.00 per month to the Reparation Trust Fund which to help different reparation processes.

vii.   Promote individual economic empowerment through skill training as well as micro-credit schemes, as in Sierra Leone (Sierra Leonean TRC, 2004).

viii.   Training and schemes target the women such as women ex-combatants, internally displaced women, war widows and all the war victims should also be included in these training and schemes. Training in basic business management courses so that trained people can establish their own small businesses (Sierra Leonean TRC, 2004).

The '6R' Recommendations

In summary, the recommendations of this book fit under the 6Rs, as detailed below.

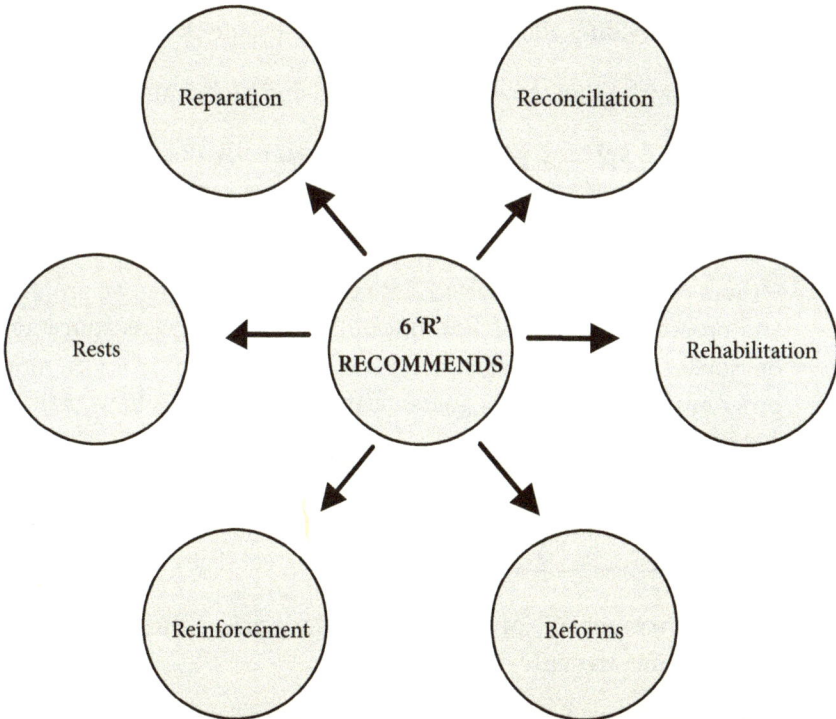

Figure 1: 6 'R' Recommendations for Nepali TRC

1. Reparation-

Trust fund, skill based training, health, pensions, education and skills training, micro-credit initiatives, community and symbolic reparations, public apology, victim or family to receive a $15,000.00 once off payment.

2. Reconciliation-

Social and cultural system, prevention of gross human rights, new social engineering (national vision), violations in future (protection of human rights), national reconciliation day, distribution and reform of land, economic, social and cultural rights, women's right, child rights.

3. Rehabilitation-

Victims' family- Unlawful detention victims have to be provided help, life skills training, job opportunities, education, health.

Children- Offering the Scholarship (free education up to university).

Widow- Providing allowance, job opportunity, life skills training.

Orphan- Managing the education, health and protection.

Internally displaced people (IDPs) / externally displaced people (EDPs)- The real victims whose property was seized, destroyed so that they were displaced should be provided help.

Others- Health related services, community development projects and programs e.g. school, health facilities, roads, women's education on small business management for sustainability, micro-economic programs and government guaranteed lending schemes to women.

4. Reforms in Rules and Regulations-

For organization, administration, and management of the country legal and judicial systems, establishment of rule of law, good governance.

5. Reinforcement of recommendations/ Running the recommendations strongly-

Implement the recommendations strongly and efficiently.

6.   Rests-

i)   Political parties and politicians-

New political culture, civil and political rights, decentralization of political powers should be developed by all the political parties and politicians.

ii)   Private organizations-

Business, media and bar association, faith communities should develop programs to help victims.

iii)   Individuals-

Every individual should develop a sense of responsibility towards the nation.

iv)   Diasporas-

Ask for cash support of at least $ 30.00 every month from each Diaspora.

v)   Related matters of TRC-

Archiving commission material and public access; follow-up committee for one year, protection for TRC commissioners, and strong punishment for breach of confidentiality in TRC matters.

AT LAST

Basically, this study intensively explored the causes and consequences of the People's War (Maoist insurgency) in Nepal as well as the procedures to provide justice to the victims and the perpetrators so that they can live together peacefully in same society. Hence, Nepali TRC could learn the lessons and follow the procedures from the strength and weaknesses of the TRCs from the case studies to complete its tasks.

However, the TRC of Nepal is in the preliminary stage of its function i.e.; it has just completed the collection of complaints from the victims and perpetrators although its two-year tenure was completed without any real progress so was extended one more year in February 2017 (My Republica, 2017). The mandates of the TRC were to find the truth of human rights violations, recommendation for the punishment of guilty, recommendation for reparation, reconciliation and rehabilitation as well as the recommendations for the reformation of the legal and institutional laws, rules and regulations of the country to avoid the repetition of the human rights violations.

For these different major tasks, the Nepali TRC should follow the other TRCs functions and recommendations which would help significantly to progress the TRC and establish the peace in Nepal. As such, after the collection of the complaints from the victims and perpetrators, the hearing process should be conducted in major parts of the country but should cover all the complainants to find the reality of human right violations and the root causes of People's War as in Liberia, Sierra Leone, and South Africa. Unless the TRC of Nepal functions in proper and effective ways, it will not accomplish its mandate to provide justice to the victims and perpetrators and will not help to establish peace successfully in Nepal.

Bibliography

Abdullah, I. (1998), 'Bush path to destruction: the origin and character of the Revolutionary United Front/Sierra Leone', The Journal of Modern African Studies, Vol. 36, No. 2, pp. 203-235.

Aboagye, F. B. (1999), ECOMOG: A sub-regional experience in conflict management and peace keeping in Liberia, Accra: Sedco

Abraham, A. (1974), Bai Bureh, The British, and the Hut Tax War, The International Journal of African Historical Studies, Boston University African Studies Center, Vol. 7, No. 1, pp. 99–106. JSTOR 216556

Abrokwaa, Dr. C. K. (n.d.), Ethnicity, Politics and Social Conflict: The Quest for Peace in

Liberia, Pennsylvania State University

Accra (2003), Comprehensive Peace Agreement, 18 August 2003, Liberia, Retrieved from

http://www.iansa.org/...Liberia-comprehensive_peace_agreement.doc

Acharya, K. (2005), An Assessment of Economic Cost of the Ongoing Armed Conflict in Nepal (An Empirical Examination of the Period 1990-2005). A Paper presented in the NEFAS/FES Seminar on Cost of Armed Conflict in Nepal organized in Kathmandu on 29-30 September 2005.

Adams, M., Bradbury, M. (1995), Conflict and Development: Background Paper for UNICEF/NGO Workshop, New York: United Nations

Adebajo, A. (2002), Liberia's Civil War, Boulder, CO: Lynne Rienner

Adebajo, A. (2002), Building peace in West Africa: Liberia, Sierra Leone and Guinea-Bissau, International peace academy occasional paper series, London: Lynne Rienner

Alao, A. (1999), *Peace Keepers, Politicians, and Warlords: the Liberian Peace Process*, New York: United Nations University Press

Amnesty International (1992), *South Africa: Torture, Ill-treatment and Executions in ANC Camps,* AFR 53/27/92, London: Amnesty International

Amnesty Committee (1994), http://www/truth.org.za/amnesty.htm on April 14, 1999, and also http://www.usip.org/library/truth. html#south_africa

Amnesty International (2004), *Morocco/Western Sahara: Amnesty International Welcomes Public Hearings into Past Violations,* London: Amnesty International

Amnesty International (2007), *Nepal: Reconciliation does not mean impunity- A memorandum on the Truth and Reconciliation Commission Bill,* Kathmandu: Amnesty International

Amnesty International (2004), *Haiti: Perpetrators of past abuses threaten human rights and the reestablishment of the rule of law,* London: Amnesty International, retrieved from http:www.amnesty.org/fr/library/info/AMR36/013/2004

Amnesty International (2004), *Morocco/Western Sahara: Amnesty International Welcomes Public Hearings into Past Violations,* London: Amnesty International, retrieved from http://www.amnesty.org/en/library/info/MDE29/010/2004

Amnesty International (2006), *Truth, Justice and Reparation: Memorandum on truth and Reconciliation Act 2006,* Liberia: Amnesty International, retrieved from http://www.amnesty.org/en/library/info/AFR34/005/2006

Amnesty International (2009), Annual Report: South Africa, retrieved from http://report2009.amnesty.org/en/regions/africa/south-africa

Amnesty International (2012), *Reconciliation at a crossroads: Continuing impunity, arbitrary detentions, torture and enforced disappearances,* Sri Lanka, Amnesty International Submission to the UN Universal Periodic Review, 1 April 2012; Amnesty International, (2012), *No Real Will to Account: Shortcomings in Sri Lanka's National Plan of Action to implement the recommendations of the LLRC*, 30 August 2012, ASA 37/010/2012

Amowitz, L. et. al. (2002), *Prevalence of war-related sexual violence and other human rights abuses among internally displaced persons in Sierra Leone*, Journal of the American Medical Association, Vol. 287, No. 4, pp. 513–521

Anderson, L. D. (2014). *Nepal's Truth and Reconciliation Commission: revised, but revitalized?* Open Democracy: 16 June 2014, retrieved from https://www.opendemocracy.net/opensecurity/liam-d-anderson/nepals-truth-and-reconciliation-commission-revised-but-revitalized

ANFREL (2013), *Nepal 2013 Constituent Assembly Election: Final report*, Thailand, Asian Network for Free ElectionAning et al (2010), *Compendium of ECOWAS peace and security decisions*, ACCRA: KAIPTC

Aning, K., & Jaye, T. (2011), *Liberia: A briefing paper on the TRC report*, Ghana: Kofi Annan International Peacekeeping Training Centre, KAIPTC occasional papper No. 33, April 2011

Annapurna Post (2005), *News*, Kathmandu: Annapurna Post, July 7 & 29

APT (n.d.), *Truth commissions: Can they prevent further violations?*, Geneva, Association for the prevention of TortureArgentine National Commission on Disappeared (1984), *Nunca Mas: The Report of the Argentine National Commission on the Disappeared*, London/ Boston: Faber & Faber

ARP (1986), *The revolution in South Africa*, Azanian Research Project, May 1986

Ash, T. G. (1997), *True confessions*, New York: Review of books. 49: 17/7: 33-38.

Attafuah, K.A. (2004), *An overview of Ghana's National Reconciliation Commission and its relationship with the courts*, Criminal Law Forum 15, N. 1-2, pp. 125-134

Augustine, S.J.P. (2010), *Community-based restorative transitional justice in Sierra Leone*, Contemporary Justice Review, 13:1, 95-119, DOI: 10.1080/10282580903343134

Avruch, K. & Vejarano, B. (2001), *Truth and Reconciliation Commissions: A Review Essay and Annotated Bibliography*, SOCIAL JUSTICE: Anthropology, Peace, and Human Rights. Volume 2(1-2):47-108.

Avruch K. & Vejarano, B.(2002), *Truth and Reconciliation Commission: A Review Essay and Annotated Bibliography*, OJPCR 4: 2: 37-76(2002) retrieved from http://www.trinstitute.org/ojpcr/4_2recon. pdfBaldwin-Ragaven et al (1999), *An ambulance of the wrong colour: Health professionals, human rights and ethics in South Africa*, Juta and Company Limited, p. 18

Ball, J. (1994), *The ritual of the necklace*, Centre for the study of violence and reconciliation, March 1994

Ball, P. (1996), *Who Did What to Whom? Planning and Implementing a Large-Scale Human*

Rights Data Project, Washington DC, USA: AAAS

Bandura, A. (2003), *"The origins and consequences of moral disengagement: A social learning perspective"*, In: F. M. Moghaddam; A. J. Marsella (eds.). *Understanding Terrorism:Psychosocial Roots, Consequences, and Interventions*, Washington DC: American Psychological Association

Baniya, J. (2007), A Masters dissertation on *'Empowering Dalits in Nepal:Lessons from South Korean NGOs' strategies*, Graduate school of International studies, Ajou University

Baral, L. R. (2006), *"Maoist Insurgency: A Prognostic Analysis"*. In L. R. Baral (ed), *Nepal: Facets of Maoist Insurgency*, New Delhi: Adroit, pp. 185- 209.

Bascom, L. C. (2009), Voices of the African American Experience, London: Greenwood Press

Basnett, Y. (2009), *From politicization of grievances to political violence: An analysis of the Maoist movement in Nepal*, London: London school of Economics and Political Science

Basoglu, M, Jaranson, J., Mollica,R., Kastrup, M.(1998), *Torture and it's consequences*, National Institute of Mental Health

Bastola, Y. (2012), *Political transition in Nepal and the role of the International community*, Transcend media service, 9 Jan 2012, retrieved from https://www.transcend.org/tms/2012/01/political-transition-in-nepal-and-the-role-of-the-international-community/

BBC News (2006*)*, *"Nepal Maoist rebels declare truce"*. BBC News. 27 April 2006.

_____, *"Nepal calls ceasefire with rebels"*. BBC News. 3 May 2006.

_____, *"Peace deal ends Nepal's civil war"*. BBC News. 21 November 2006.

BBC News (2008), "Prachanda's first interview as Nepal PM". BBC News. 3 September 2008.

BBC News (2009), *"Country profile: Liberia"* retrieved from http://news.bbc.co.uk/2/hi/africa/country_ profiles/1043500.stm.

BBC News (2009), "Whose Justice? Liberia, retrieved from http://news.bbc.co.uk/2/hi/programmes/newsnight/7861430.stm#3

BBC News (2013), *Apartheid's roots: The native land act*, retrieved from http://www.bbc.co.uk/history/0/22786616

BBC News (2013), *Nepal's Colonel Kumar Lama charged in UK with torture*, 5 Jan 2013, retrieved from http://www.bbc.com/news/world-asia-20914282

BBC News (2015), *Nepal blockade: six ways it affects the country*, 12 Dec 2015, retrieved from http://www.bbc.com/news/world-asia-35041366

BBC and NNBN (2014), *Civil Society Report on Beijing+20 Nepal,* November 2014.

Beer de, A. S., Fouché, J. (2000), *In search of truth: the TRC and the South African press – a case study,* Ecquid Novi: African Journalism Studies, 21/2: 190-206.

Bellows, J. & Miguel, E.(2006), *War and institutions: new evidence from Sierra Leone,* The American Economic Review, Vol. 96, No. 2, pp. 394–399.

Betancourt T. S. et al (2010). *Past horrors, present struggles: the role of stigma in the association between war experiences and psychosocial adjustment among former child soldiers in Sierra Leone.* Soc. Sci. Med. 70, 17–26 10.1016/j.socscimed.2009.09.038 [PMC free article] [PubMed] [Cross Ref]

Bhattachan, Y. K. (2001), *"Peace and Good Governance in Nepal: The Socio-cultural Context."* pp. 73-88. In Quest For Peace. SAP-Nepal, Kathmandu: South Asia Partnership-Nepal

Bhattachan et al (2009), *Caste-based discrimination in Nepal,* working paper series Vol 3, No. 08, New Delhi: Indian Institute Of Dalit Studies

Bhatta, C.D. (2012), *Reflections on Nepal's Peace Process,* Germany: Friedrich-Ebert-Stiftung

Bhatta, C.D. (2013), *Nepal: Antinomies of Democracy, Peace and External Influence,* Kathmandu, Telegraphnepal.com, retrieved from http://www.telegraphnepal.com/views/2013-06-13/nepal:-antinomies-of-democracy-peace-and-external-influence

Bhattarai et al (2004), *Statistics of Tourism-2004,* Kathmandu: Government of Nepal

Bloomfield et al (2003), *Reconciliation after violent conflict,* A handbook, Stockholm: International IDEA

Bones, A. (2001), *"Case Study: Peacekeeping in Sierra Leone,"* pp. 55-64 in *Human Security and the New Diplomacy: Protecting People, Promoting Peace,* (eds). McRae, R. & Hubert, D., Montreal, McGill-Queen's University Press

Boraine, A., Levy, J., & Scheffer, R., (eds) (1994), *Dealing with the past: Truth and Reconciliation in South Africa,* Cape Town: ADASA

Boraine, A. (2000), *A country unmasked: Inside South Africa's Truth and Reconciliation Commission,* Oxford, New York: Oxford University Press

Brahm, E. (2004), *Truth Commissions: Beyond Intractability*, (Eds.) Guy Burgess, G. & Burgess, H., *Conflict Information Consortium*, University of Colorado, Boulder, June 2004 retrieved from http://www.beyondintractability.org/essay/truth-commissions

Brahm, E. (2004), Truth Commissions, retrieved from http://www.intractableconflict.org/m/truth_commissions.jsp#top

Bronkhorst, D. (2006) *Truth and Justice: A Guide to Truth Commissions and Transitional*

Justice 6, 2d. ed., Amnesty International

Buergenthal, T. (1994), *The United Nations Truth Commission for El Salvador*, Vanderbilt Journal of Transnational Law 27, No. 3: 497

Burman M. E., McKay S. (2007), *Marginalization of girl mothers during reintegration from armed groups in Sierra Leone.* Int. Nurs. Rev. 54, pp. 316–323 10.1111/j.1466-7657.2007.00546.x [PubMed][Cross Ref]

Capoccia, G., Kelemen, R.D. (2007), *"The Study of Critical Junctures Theory, Narrative, and Counterfactuals in Historical Institutionalism,"* World Politics, Vol. 59 (April 2007), pp. 341–69.

Caritas Nepal (2005), *Caravan of IDPs.* Kathmandu: Caritas Nepal

Carver, R. (1990), *Called to Account: How African Governments Investigate Human Rights Violations,* African Affairs 89, No. 356 (July, 1, 1990), pp. 391-415

CCD (2009), *Participatory Constitution making process, booklet series No. 10,* Centres for Constitutional Dialogue

CIDA (n.d.), *Truth and reconciliation commissions: Operational framework,* Canada: Canadian International Development Agency

Clark, J. N. (2008), The three Rs: retributive justice, restorative justice, and reconciliation, Contemporary justice review, vol. 11, No. 4, pp. 331-350, doi.org/10.1080/10282580802482603

Clarke, K. (2011), *The Rule of Law Through Its Economies of Appearances: The Making of the African Warlord,* Indiana Journal of Global Legal Studies, Vol. 18, No. 1 (Winter 2011)

Cochran-Budhathoki, K., & Worden, S. (2007), *Transitional Justice in Nepal: A Look at the International Experience of Truth Commissions*, USA: United States Institute of Peace, 1 September 2007 retrieved from http://www.usip.org/publications/transitional-justice-in-nepal-look-the-international-experience-of-truth-commissions

Collier, P., & Sambanis, S. (2002), *"Understanding civil war: A new agenda"*, The Journal of Conflict Resolution, Vol. 46, No. 1, pp. 3-12.

Commission for reception, Truth and Reconciliation in East Timor (CAVR), retrieved from http://www.cavr-timorleste.org/, accessed on 24 June 2015

Connolly, C. K. (2006), *Living on the Past: The Role of Truth Commissions in Post-Conflict Societies and the Case Study of Northern Ireland*, 39 Cornell Intl. L.J. 401, 410 (2006).

Cook, N. (2003), *Liberia: 1989-1997 civil war, Post-war developments and US relations*, Liberia: Congressional Research Service

CPA Article (2006), *Comprehensive Peace Accord-2006*, Kathmandu: Government of Nepal

Crisis Group (2006), *The report: 2006*, Kathmandu: Crisis Group

CSVR (n.d.), *Justice in Perspective- Truth and Justice Commission*, Africa- Chad: Center for the Study of Violence and Reconciliation, retrieved from http://www.justiceinperspective.org.za/index.php?option=com_content&task=view&id=8&Itemid=19, accessed 25 June 2015

Cuya, E. (1996), *Las Comisiones De La Verdad En America Latina, Ko'Aga Rone'Eta iii,* retrieved from http://www.derechos.org/koaga/iii/1/cuya.html

Daalder, I., & O'Hanlon, M. (2000), *The Roots of the War, June 2000,retrieved from* FrontlinePBS.org,http://www.pbs.org/wgbh/pages/frontline/shows/kosovo/readings/roots.html

Dahal, D. R. (2006), *Civil Society Groups in Nepal: Their Roles in Conflict and Peace building,* Kathmandu: Support for Peace and Development Initiative (UNDP), p. 27

Davis, S.M. (1987), *Apartheid's Rebels: Inside South Africa's Hidden War*, New Haven, CT: Yale University Press

Davis, F. J. (1991), *Who is Black? One Nation's Definition*, University Park, PA: Pennsylvania State University Press

DeMinck, A., (2007), *The Origins of Truth and Reconciliation Commissions: South Africa,*

Sierra Leone, and Peru, Honors Projects, Paper 8. 2007, retrieved from http://digitalcommons.macalester.edu/soci_honors/8

Deng, W. D. (2001), *A Survey of Programs on the Reintegration of Former Child Soldiers,* Liberia: Country Profile, 30 March 2001, online at: http://www.mofa.go.jp/policy/human/child/survey/profile3.html

DLRM Nepal (2016), *Land Act 2012,* Nepal: Department of Land Reform and Management, Nepal

Deraniyagala, S. (2005), *The political economy of civil conflict in Nepal,* Oxford development studies, Vol. 33, No. 1, pp. 47-62

DeRouen, K. & Heo., U. (2007), *Civil Wars of the World: Major Conflicts Since World War II,* Santa Barbara: ABC-CLIO, Vol. 1

Devarajan, S. (2005), *South Asian Surprises,* Keynote speech at the World Bank/ IMF/DFID conference on Macroeconomic Policy Challenges in Low Income Countries. Washington DC, Feb. 15-16, 2005.

Dhruba K., (2005) *Impact of Conflict on Security and the Future: The Case of Nepal,* Nepal: Tribhuvan University

Dhungana, S.K., (2006) (ed), *The Maoist Insurgency and Nepal-India Relations,* Kathmandu, Friends For Peace Publications, Series 010, p.7.

Do and Iyer (2007), *Poverty, social divisions and conflict in Nepal,* World Bank policy research paper 4228

Dolo, E. (1996), *Democracy versus Dictorship,* New York: University Press of America

Dong-Choon, K., Selden, M. (2010), *South Korea's Embattled Truth and reconciliation Commission,* The Asia-Pacific Journal: Japan Focus,

7 March 2010, retrieved http://www.japanfocus.org/-Kim-Dong_choon/3313

Dougherty, B. K., (2004), *Searching for answers: Sierra Leone's Truth & Reconciliation Commission,* African Studies Quarterly, Vol. 8, No. 1: 39-56

Doyle, M. W., & Nicholas, S. N. (2006), *Making War and Building Peace: United Nations Peace Operations,* Princeton and Oxford: Princeton University Press

Dumbuya, L. (2003), *The TRC in post conflict Sierra Leone,* Egypt: The American University in Cairo

Dyzenhaus, D. (2000), *Justifying the Truth and reconciliation commission,* Toronto: The journal of Political Philosophy, Vol. 8, No. 4, 2000, pp. 470-496

ECN (2013), *The result of election 2013,* Kathmandu: Election Commission Nepal

Elliot, J. (2015), *Nepal earthquake deaths: Blame weak, corrupt, politicians,* Newsweek, retrieved from http://www.newsweek.com/nepal-earthquake-deaths-blame-weak-corrupt-politicians-325530

El Pais (1985), *"Alfonsin decreta estado sitio"* on 26 Oct 1985 (in Spanish)

Eschborm (2002), *Nepal Country Study on Conflict Transformation and Peace Building,* German Organization for Technical Cooperation (GTZ)

Engdahl, B & Fairbank, J.(1998), *Former Prisoners of War: Highlights of Empirical Research' in National Institute of Mental Health,* March 1998

Faber & Faber (1986), *Nunca Mas: The report of the Argentine National Commission on the Disappeared,* London & Boston: Argentine National Commission on Disappeared

Farar, Strauss, Giroux (1986), *Nunca Mas: The Report of the Argentine National Commission on the disappeared,* New York: Argentine National Commission on Disappeared

Farasat, W. & Hayner, P. (2009), *Negotiating peace in Nepal: Implications for justice*, Brussels: ICTJ

Florentin, B., Manuel, J. (2006), *Commission De Verdad Justicia Del Paraguay y La Luncha Antiterrorista*, Buenos Aires, retrieved from http://ejp.icj.org/IMG/BenitezFlorentin.pdf

Fombad, C. M. (2008), *Transitional justice in Africa: The experience with Truth commissions*, Hauser Global law School Program, New York University of Law, available at www.nyulawglobal.org/Globalex/Africa_Truth_Commissions.htm

Foster et al (2009), *A house with two rooms*, USA: Dispute Resolution Institute Press

Fowler, W. (2004), *Operation Barras*, London: Weidenfeld & Nicholson.

Fyle, C.M. (2006), *Historical dictionary of Sierra Leone*, USA: Scarecrow press

Galtung, J. (1964), *An editorial, Journal of Peace research*, 1 (1), 1-4

Galtung, J. (1969), *"Violence, peace and peace research"*, Journal of Peace Research, Vol. 6, No. 3, pp. 167-191.

Galtung, J.; Tschudi, F. (2001), *"Crafting peace: On the psychology of the transcend approach"*, In: D. J. Christie; R. V. Wagner; D. A. Winter (eds.). *Peace, Conflict, and Violence*. Upper Saddle River, NJ: Prentice-Hall, pp. 210-222

Galtung, J. (1996), *Peace by Peaceful Means: Peace and conflict, development and civilisation*, Oslo: PRIO

Gautam, S.; Banskota A.; Manchanda, R. (2001), *"Where there are no men: Women in the Maoist insurgency in Nepal"*, In: R. Manchanda (ed.). *Women, War and Peace in South Asia: Beyond Victimhood to Agency*. New Delhi: Sage Publications, pp. 214-51.

Gberie, L (2005), *A dirty war in West Africa: The RUF and the destruction of Sierra Leone*, Bloomington: Indiana University Press

Gberie, L. (2015), *War, Politics and Justice in West Africa Essays 2003-2014*, Sierra Leone: Osman San Koh (Mallan O.)

Gentilucci, G., (2005), *Truth-Telling and Accountability in Democratizing Nations: The Cases Against Chile's Agusto Pinochet and South Korea's Chun Doo-Hwan and Roh Tae-Woo,* Connecticut Public Interest Law Journal, 2005:5

Gerrity, E., Keane, T.M., Tuma, F. (2001), *The Mental Health Consequences of Torture and Related Violence and Trauma,* National Institute of Mental Health, New York: Plenum Publishers

Gersony, R. (2003), *Sowing the wind: History and dynamics of the Maoist revolt in Nepal's Rapti Hills.* Mercy Corps International/USAID report.

Ghimire, Y. (2006), *"The Many Dimensions of Nepali Insurgency,"* in Building a CATR Research Agenda, Proceedings of the Third Annual International Symposium of the Center for Asian Terrorism Research (CATR) March 1-3, 2006, Colombo, Sri Lanka, IDA Paper P-4163

Ghimire, Y. (2012), *An inglorious trip,* Spotlight Nepal, Vol:6, No. 13

Gibson, J.L. (2006). The contributions of truth to reconciliation: Lessons from South Africa. *Journal of Conflict Resolution, 50*(3), Transitional Justice (Jun, 2006), pp.409–432.Sage publication

GICHD (2015), *National capabilities and residual contamination Nepal,* Geneva: Geneva International Centre for Humanitarian Demining

Goldstone, R. J. (1996), *Justice as a Tool for Peacemaking: Truth Commissions and International Criminal Tribunals,* New York University Journals of International Law and Politics, 1996:28 GoN (2015), *Nepal Tourism Statistics-2015,* Kathmandu: Government of Nepal, Ministry of Culture, Toursim and Civil Aviation

Gonzalez, E. (2013), *Drafting a truth commission mandate: A practical tool,* New York: International centre for transitional justice (ICTJ)

Gorkhapatra (2014), *Daily News: 29 March 2014,* Kathmandu: Gorkhapatra Sansthan

GoSA (1995), *Government Gazette No. 16885,* Cape Town: Government of South Africa

Government of Liberia (2005), *TRC Act 2005,* retrieved from www. trcofliberia.org

GoN (2006), *Full text of the Comprehensive Peace Agreement held between Government of Nepal and Communist Party of Nepal (Maoist)*, Kathmandu: Government of Nepal

GoN (2011), *Report of IDP Registration at relief and reconstruction division*, Kathmandu: Government of Nepal

GoN (2011), *Shadow report on the fourth and fifth periodic report of the Government of Nepal on CEDAW*, Kathmandu

GoN (2015), *Constitution of Nepal*, Kathmandu: Government of Nepal

Graybill, L.S. (2002), *TRC in S Africa: Miracle or Model?*, Boulder, Colorado: Lynne Rienner Publishers

Greiff, P. D. (2006), *The handbook of reparations*, New York: Oxford university press

GTZ (2010), *GTZ's report ⊠Towards peace: The Maoist Army Combatants and the adjacent communities*, Kathmandu: Format Printing Press

Gurung, H, Malla K. Sunder, Krishna Bhattachan & Om Gurung (2000), *Janjati Bikasko Jukti (Ideas for Nationalities' Development)*, Kathmandu: Janjati Bikash Samanya Kemdra

Gurung, H. (2005), *"Social exclusion and Maoist insurgency"* paper presented at National Dialogue Conference on ILO Convention 169 on Indigenous and Tribal Peoples, Kathmandu, January 19-20, 2005.

Gurung, P. (2013). *A Continuous Struggle for Transitional Justice through Truth and Reconciliation: A case study of enforcedly disappeared in Nepal*

Gyawali, T.R. (2009), *Socio-Economic Impact of Political Insurgency in Nepal,*   Japan: Maeda Corporation

Hachhethu, K. (2004), *The Nepali state and the Maoist insurgency, 1996-2001*, In Hutt, M. (2004), *Himalayan 'People's war' Nepal's Maoist Rebellion*, London: Hurst & Company

Hachchethu (2005), *Maoist Insurgency in Nepal: An overview, retrieved from* www.uni-bielefeld.de/midea/pdf/harticle2.pdf

Hachhethu, K. (2014), *Why Nepal might not have a constitution on 22 January 2015*, retrieved from http://www.constitutionnet.org/news/why-nepal-might-not-have-constitution-22-january-2015

Hada, J. (2001), *Housing and squatter settlements. In city diagnostic report for city development strategy*, Kathmandu: Kathmandu metropolitan city/The World Bank

Hamal, C. (2013), *PLA fighters finally become NA personnel,* Kathmandu: República Nepal, 5 July 2013

Hayner, P.B. (1994), *Fifteen Truth Commissions–1974 to 1994: A Comparative Study*, Human Rights Quarterly, Vol. 16, No. 4, November 1994, pp. 597-655

Hayner, P.B. (2001), *Unspeakable Truths: Confronting State Terror & Atrocity*, New York: Routledge, 2001

Hayner, P. (2001), *Unspeakable Truths: Facing the Challenges of Truth Commissions,* New York: Routledge.

Hayner, P. (2004), *The Sierra Leone truth and reconciliation commission: Reviewing the first year,* ICTJ

Hayner, P. (2007), *Negotiating Peace in Liberia: Preserving the Possibility for Justice,*

International Center for Transitional Justice, November (2007)

Heston et al (2002), *Penn world tables*, Version 6.1, Centre for international comparisons at the university of Pennsylvania (CICUP)

Himalayan Times (2005), *News*, Kathmandu: Himalayan Times, 10 July 2005

Hirsch, J. L. (2001), *Sierra Leone: Diamonds and the Struggle for Democracy*, Boulder: Lynne Rienner, 2001

Hossain, M., Siitonen, L. & Sharma, S. (2006), *Development Cooperation for conflict prevention and conflict resolution*, Helsinki: Institute of Development Institute, University of Helsinki

Human Rights Commission,(1990), *Violence in Detention*, People and Violence in South Africa, Oxford University Press, 1990

HRW (2000), *Sierra Leone Rebels Forcefully Recruit Child Soldiers*, New York: Human Rights Watch

HRW (2000), *Sierra Leone: Priorities for the international community*, New York: Human Rights Watch

HRW (2003), *We'll kill you if you cry: Sexual violence in the Sierra Leone conflict*, New York: Human Rights Watch

HRW (2008), *Report: 2008*, Kathmandu: Human Rights Watch

HRW (2010), *Report: 2010*, Kathmandu: Human Rights Watch

HRW (2013), *We Will Teach You a Lesson - Sexual Violence against Tamils by Sri Lankan Security Forces*, 26 February 2013, Human Rights Watch, ISBN: 1-56432-993-3, retrieved from http://www.unhcr.org/refworld/docid/5130850f2.html.HRW (2014), *Whose development? Human rights abuses in Sierra Leone's mining booms*, Human Rights Watch

Hutt, M. (2004), *Himalayan People's War: Nepal's Maoist rebellion*, London: C. Hurst & Co.

Hutt, M. (2004), *Introduction: Monarchy, Democracy and Maoism in Nepal*, In: Hutt, M., (ed.), *Himalayan 'People's War': Nepal's Maoist Rebellion*, Bloomington: Indiana University Press, Hurst & Company

Hudson, R. A. (1999), *"The Sociology and Psychology of Terrorism: Who Becomes a Terrorist and Why?"* A report prepared under an interagency agreement by the Federal Research Division, Library of Congress, Washington DC: Federal Research Division, Library of Congress

ICG, (2007*), Nepal's peace agreement: making it work*, International Crisis Group

ICG (2009), *Liberia: Uneven Progress in Security Sector Reform*, International Crisis Group

ICG (2011), *Nepal's fitful peace process*, Kathmandu/Brussels: International Crisis Group, Asia briefing No. 120, 7 April 2011

ICG (2013), *Sri Lanka's Authoritarian Turn: The Need for International Action*, 20 February 2013, International Crisis Group, Asia Report N°243, available at: http://www.unhcr.org/refworld/docid/5124deb32.html

ICTJ (2009), *Transitional justice and DDR: The case of S. Africa*, Finland, International Centre for Transitional Justice

ICTJ (2010), *Across the lines: The impact of Nepal's conflict on women*, International Centre for Transitional Justice

ICTJ (2010), *Sierra Leone*, UN Human rights council, International Centre for Transitional Justice

ICTJ (2014), *Can Truth Commissions strengthen peace processes?* Finland: International Centre for Transitional Justice

ICTJ (2014), *Challenging the conventional: Can Truth commissions strengthen peace processes?* Finland: International Centre for Transitional Justice

ICTJ (2016), *Nepal government fails to bring laws for operation of TRC and CIEDP*, Kathmandu, 28 April 2016, International Centre for Transitional Justice, retrieved from https://www.ictj.org/news/nepal-government-fails-bring-laws-operation-trc-and-ciedp

IDMC, I. (2006). *Sudan: Slow IDP return to south while Darfur crisis continues unabated,* Norwegian Refugee Council

IJRC (2013), Truth and Reconciliation Commission for Nepal continues to face criticism, International Justice Resource Centre (IJRC)

Ilic, D. (2004), *The Yugoslav truth and reconciliation commission*, Eurozine, 23 April 2004, pp. 1-22.

ILO (2005), *Dalits and Labour in Nepal: Discriminations and Forced Labour*, Kathmandu: ILO Office Nepal

INSEC (2013), *Truth and reconciliation regimes: Reflection and relevance- A case study of Nepal,* Kathmandu: Informal Sector service Centre (INSEC)

IRIN (2006), *Between Two Stones: Nepal's Decade Long Civil War*, Integrated Regional Information NetworksJackson, P. & Albrecht, P. (2010*), Security sector reform in Sierra Leone 1997-2007: Views from the front line,* Geneva, Geneva centre for the democratic control of armed forces (DCAF)

James-Allen, P. et al. (2003), *Sierra Leone's TRC and special court: A citizen's handbook*, ICTJ and National Forum for Human Rights

James-Allen, P., Weah, A. & Goodfriend, L. (2010), *Beyond the truth and reconciliation commission: Transitional justice options in Liberia,* Liberia: International Centre for Transitional Justice (ICTJ)

Jaye, T. (2009), *Transitional justice and DDR: The case of Liberia,* Liberia: International Centre for Transitional Justice (ICTJ)

Jha, H.B. (2010), *A Rapid Situation Assessment on Agriculture and Migration in Nepal,* Kathmandu: Centre for Economic and Technical Studies, p. 27.

Jha, H.B. (2011), *The Economics of Peace: A Nepalese Perspective,* ORF Occasional Paper # 29, December 2011, New Delhi: Observer Research Foundation, p. 14.

Jones, E. (2007), *Post-Combat Disorders: The Boer War to the Gulf,* War and Health, 5-39.

Joshi, M., Mason, T. (2007), *Land Tenure, Democracy and Insurgency in Nepal: Peasant Support for Insurgency versus Democracy in Nepal,* Asian Survey, Vol. 47, No. 3, pp. 393-414Kaifala, J. (2017), *Free slaves, Freetown, and the Sierra Leonean civil war,* New York, Macmillan

Kaldor, M. & Vincent, J. (2006), *Case study sierra Leone,* New York: United Nations Development Programme

Kantipur (2015), *Formation of Truth and Reconciliation Commission and The Commission on Enforced Disappearances,* Kathmandu: Kantipur News on 10 Feb 2015

Kantipur (12015), *TRC has been formed to restore justice system, reconcile society,* Kantipur News on 16 Feb 2015, retrieved from http://kathmandupost.ekantipur.com/news/2015-02-16/trc-has-been-formed-to-restore-justice-system-reconcile-society.html

Kantipur (2016), *Government apathy leaves TRC in quandary,* Kantipur News on 14 Nov 2016, retrieved from http://kathmandupost.ekantipur.com/news/2016-11-14/govt-apathy-leaves-trc-in-a-quandary.html

Karkee, M. (2008), *Nepal economic growth assessment Agriculture,* Kathmandu: USAID Nepal

Karki & Bhattarai (eds.) (2003), *Whose War? Economic and Socio-Cultural Impacts of Nepal's Maoist-Government Conflict,* Kathmandu: NGO Federation of Nepal

Karki, A. & Seddon, D. (2003), *The People's War in Nepal – Left Perspective,* New Delhi: Adroit Publishers

Katsiaficas, G. (2013), *Asia's unknown uprisings,* CA: PM Press, Vol. 2

Keen, D. (2003), *Greedy Elites, Dwindling Resources, Alienated Youths: The Anatomy of Protracted Violence in Sierra Leone,* Internationale Politik und Gesellschaft, Vol. 2, retrieved from http://www.fes.de/ipg/IPG2_2003/ARTKEEN.HTM

Keen, D. (2005), *Conflict and collusion in Sierra Leone,* Oxford, James Currey/Palgrave Macmillan; ISBN: 9781403967183

Kelly, P. (2009), *Email,* U.S. Embassy in Nepal

Kelsall, T. (2009), *Culture under cross-examination: International justice and the special court for Sierra Leone,* Cambridge: Cambridge university press

Killson, M. (1966) *Political Change in a West African State: A Study of the Modernization Process in Sierra Leone,* Cambridge, Massachusetts, USA, pp. 60; also pp. 106, 107, 110, 111, 186–188 on other riots and strikes.

Kim, H. (2012), *Truth and reconciliation Commission, Republic of Korea,* (eds.) Stan, L. & Nedelsky, N. in *The Encyclopedia of Transitioal Justice,* Cambridge: Cambridge University Press

King, I., & Mason, W. (2006), *Peace at any Price: How the World failed Kosovo.* New York: Cornell University Press

Kreuttner, T. R. (2001), *The Maoist Insurgency in Nepal, 1996-2008: Implications for U.S. Counterinsurgency Doctrine,* USA

Kreuttner, T.R., (2013), *The Maoist Insurgency in Nepal and US Counterinsurgency Doctrine,* Smallwars Journal, Small Wars Foundation

Kumar, D. (2003), *"Consequences of the militarized conflict and the cost of violence in Nepal",* Contributions to Nepalese Studies, Vol. 30, No. 2, pp. 167-216

Kumarasamy, S. (2012), *Critical examination of the truth and reconciliation process in post-conflict Sri Lanka,* Alberta: Athabasca University

Laakso, J. (2003), *In Pursuit of Truth, Justice and Reconciliation: The Truth Commissions of East Timor and South Africa,* Social Alternatives, 2003: 22(2)

Lahai, J. I. & Lyons, T. (2015), *African Frontiers: Insurgency, governance and Peace building in Postcolonial states,* New York: Routledge Taylor and Francis group

Lamb, C. (1999), *Truth panel will call Nigeria's strongmen to account,* Electronic Telegraph, 22 August 1999

Larry, D. (2002), *Thinking about hybrid regimes,* Journal of Democracy, Vol. 13, No. 2, April 2002, pp. 21-35, The Johns Hopkins University Press DOI: 10.1353/jod.2002.0025

Lawoti, M. (2005), *Towards a Democratic Nepal: Inclusive Political Institu-tion for a Multicultural Society,* New Delhi: Sage Publications

Lawoti, M. & Pahari, K. (2009), *The Maoist Insurgency in Nepal Revolution in the twenty first century,* Routledge

Leve, L. G. (2007), *"Failed development' and rural revolution in Nepal: Rethinking subaltern consciousness and women's empowerment",* Anthropological Quarterly, Vol. 80, No. 1, pp. 127-172.

Lewiston, T.J. (2003), *Issues of Sovereignty, Strategy and Security in the ECOWAS Intervention in the Liberian Civil War,* New York: Edwin Mellen Press

Liberian CPA (2003), *Article III of the Comprehensive Peace Agreement,* 18 August 2003, Government of Liberia, 18 August 2003

Liberian TRC (2003), *Final Report Volume I,* retrieved from www.trcofliberia.org

Liberian TRC (2009), *TRC Report,* retrieved form www.trcofliberia.org

Liberian TRC Act (2005), *Section 4 of Article III of the TRC Act,* TRC of Liberia, 12 May 2005

Liberian TRC Act (2005), *Article VII Section 26 of the TRC Act,* TRC of Liberia, 12 May 2005

Liberian TRC Act (2005), *Section J of the TRC Act,* TRC of Liberia, 12 May 2005

Liberian TRC Act (2005), *Section G of the TRC Act*, TRC of Liberia, 12 May 2005

Long, W. J. (2008), *Liberia's Truth and Reconciliation Commission: An interim assessment*, International Journal of Peace Studies, Vol. 13, No. 2, Autumn/Winter 2008

Lynch, C. (2004), *Rights Group Says Sudan's Government Aided Militias*, Washington Post, 20 July 2004, p. A12.

Macours, K. (2010), *Increasing inequality and civil conflict in Nepal,* Oxford Economic Papers, Vol. 63, No. 1, pp. 1-26.

Magarrell, L & Gutierrez, B. (2006), *Lessons in Truth-seeking: International experiences informing United States initiatives,* New York: International Center for transitional Justice (ICTJ) on Sept 2006

Marks, T. (2007), *Maoist People's War in Post Vietnam Asia*, 303, 304; Sharma, S. (2004), *The Maoist Movement; an Evolutionary Perspective*, in Hutt, M. (2004), *Himalayan People's War: Nepal's Maoist rebellion*, pp 42-49, London, C. Hurst & Co.

Mattarollo, R. (n.d.), *What to Expect from a Truth Commission*, retrieved from

http://www.sierra-leone.org/trcbook-rodolfomattarollo.html

Medeiros E. (2007), *Integrating mental health into post-conflict rehabilitation: the case of Sierra Leonean and Liberian "child soldiers."* J. Health Psychology, Vol. 12, pp. 498–504, 10.1177/1359105307076236

Meheta, A.K. (2004), *"Maoist Insurgency in Nepal: Implications for India"*, Bharat Rakshak Monitor, Vol. 6, No.4, Jan-Feb 2004

Mendeloff, D. (2004), *Truth-Seeking, Truth-Telling, and Postconflict Peacebuilding: Curb the Enthusiasm?*, International Studies Review, 6

Migyikra, E. N. (2008), *Truth and Reconciliation Comissions: A Comparative Sudy Of South Africa, Ghana And Sierra Leone*, Austria: European University Center for Peace Studies.

Miklian, J. (2008), *Nepal's Terai: Constructing an ethnic conflict*, Oslo: International Peace Research Institute

Millar, G. (2010), *Assessing local experiences of truth-telling in Sierra Leone: getting to 'why' through a qualitative case study analysis*, International Journal of Transitional Justice Vol. 4, No. 3, pp. 477–496

Millar, G. (2011), *Local evaluations of justice through truth telling in Sierra Leone: Postwar needs and transitional justice*, The Netherland: Radbound University, DOI 10.1007/s12142-011-0195-x

Mishra, R. (2004), *India's role in Nepal's Maoist insurgency*, Asian Survey, Vol. XLIV, No. 5, September/October

Mitchell, C. R. (1981), *The Structure of International Conflict*, London: Macmillan Press

Mngxitama, A. (2004), *In Retrospect: A Look at the 1976 Soweto Uprising*, Le Journal Des Alternatives

MoLD (2002), *Report: 2002*, Kathmandu: Ministry of Local Development

Momoh, J. (2011), *Sierra Leone: Viewpoint – Celebrating a New Nation!*, 4 May 2011, retrieved from allAfrica.com

Monama, B. (1996), *A case study on impunity: South Africa, Consultative and planning meeting for a campaign against impunity in Africa*, Ouagadougou, Burkina Faso, 22-3 March

Muni, S.D. (2003), *The Maoist Insurgency in Nepal: The Challenge and The Response.* New Delhi: Rupa and Co.

Muni, S.D. (2012), *Bringing the Maoist down from the hills: India's role*, In Einsiedel et al (ed.) *Nepal in transition: From people's war to fragile peace*, New York: Cambridge University press, pp. 313-331

Mustafa, M. & Bangura, J. J. (2010), *Sierra Leone beyond the Lome Peace Accord*, New York: Macmillan

Myers, R. (2006), *Crime Victims as Subjects of Documentaries: Exploitation or Advocacy? FORDHAM INTELL. PROP. MEDIA & ENT. L.J., 16*, 733-788.

MyRepublica (2016), *TRC, CIEDP remain idle for lack of regulations*, Kathmandu, New republic media, 16 Jan 2016, retrieved from http://

admin.myrepublica.com/politics/story/35896/trc-ciedp-remain-idle-for-lack-of-regulations.htmlNEOC (2013), *Observation of Nepal's constituent assembly election-2013*, Nepal, National Election Observation Committee

NPC (2005), *An Assessment of the Implementation of the Tenth Plan (PRSP)*, Kathmandu: National Planning Commission

National Unity and Reconciliation Commission, retrieved from http://www.nurc.gov.rw/

Naidu, E. (2004), *Symbolic reparations: A fractured opportunity*, South Africa: Centre for the study of violence and reconciliation

NBS (2005), *Report: 2005*, Nepal: Central Bureau of Statistics

Neil J. Kritz (ed.) (1995), *Transitional Justice: How Emerging Democracies Reckon with Former Regimes*, Washington D.C.: United States Institute of Peace, 3 Vols., 1995

Neil J. Kritz, (1996), *Coming to terms with Atrocities: A review of Accountability Mechanisms for Mass violations of Human Rights*, 59 LAW & CONTEM. PROBS 127

Nepal, M., Bohara, A. K., & Gawande, K. (2011), *More Inequality, More Killings: The Maoist Insurgency in Nepal*, American Journal of Political Science, Vol. 55, No. 4, pp. 886-906. doi:10.1111/j.1540-5907.2011.00529.x

Nepalekhabar (2016), *TRC submits interim report*, 7 Feb 2016, retrieved from http://nepalekhabar.com/2016/02/62977Newman, A. (2008), *Maoists set for election victory in Nepal*, Nepal, Socialist Unity, retrieved from http://socialistunity.com/maoists-set-for-election-victory-in-nepal/ Ofuatey-Kodjoe, W. (1994), *Regional organisations and the resolution of internal conflict: The ECOWAS intervention in Liberia*, International peace keeping, Vol. 1, No. 3, Autumn 1994, p. 267

Ohaegbulam, F. U. (2004), *U.S. policy in postcolonial Africa: Four case studies in conflict resolution*, New York: Peter Lang Publishing, Inc.

OHCHR (2007) Human Rights in Nepal One year after the Comprehensive Peace Agreement, Nepal: United Nations OHCHR

Ojielo, O. (2010), *Critical Lessons in Post-Conflict Security in Africa: The case of Liberia's Truth and Reconciliation Commission*

Omonijo, M. (1990), *Doe: The Liberian Tragedy*, Oregon: Sahel

Painter, R. C. (2009), *Weak state and political constraints: Experiments with truth in Liberia and Sierra Leone*, Political Science Honors Projects, Paper#20 retrieved from http://digitalcommons.macalester.edu/poli_honors/20

Pandey, N.N. (2005), *Nepal's Maoist Movement and Implications for India and China,* RCSS Policy Studies No. 27, Colombo, Manohar Publish-ersPandey, L. (2017), *TRC, CIEDP to accept complaints again,* Kathmandu: Himalaya Times, on 16 Feb 2017

Park, A. (2010), *Community-based restorative transitional justice in Sierra Leone,* Contemporary Justice Review, Vol. 13, No. 1, pp. 95-119.

Parvati, C. (2003), *Women's Participation in the People's War,* In: A. Karki; D. Seddon (eds).

Parwez, M. S. (2006), *An empirical analysis of conflict in Nepal,* Asian Development Bank Working Paper Series No. 7, on July 2006.

Pascoe, D. (2007), *Are truth and reconciliation commissions an effective means of dealing with state-organised criminality?* Cross-sections, 93-115

Pathak, B. (2005), *Politics of People's War and Human Rights in Nepal,* Kathmandu: BIMPA Publication

Pathak, B. (2015), *Enforced Disappearance Commission: Truth, Justice and Reparation for Dignity,* TRANSCEND Media Service, on 24 August 2015

Pathak, B. (2016), *World's disappearance commissions: An inhumanious quest for truth,* World Journal of Social Science research, Vol.3, No. 3 on www.scholink.org/ojs/index.php/wjssr

Patton, M. Q. (1990). *Qualitative Evaluation and Research Methods* (2nd ed.), Newbury Park, CA: Sage Publications, Inc.

Perriello, T. & Wierda, M. (2006), *The special court for Sierra Leone under scrutiny,* International Centre for Transitional Justice (ICTJ)

Pettigrew, J. & Shneiderma, S. (2004), *Women and the Maobaadi: Ideology and agency in Nepal's Maoist movement,* Himal South Asian, Vol. 17, No. 1, pp. 19-29

Pettigrew, J. (2012), *Unexpected Consequences of Everyday Life During the Maoist Insurgency in Nepal,* Journal of International Women's Studies, Vol. 13, No. 4, pp. 99-112

Pham, John-Peter (2005), *Child Soldiers, Adult Interests: The Global Dimensions of the Sierra Leonean Tragedy,* Nova Publishers. pp. 4–8. *ISBN 978-1-59454-671-6*

Pokhrel, K. (2015), *Nepal Misses Its Latest Constitution-Writing Deadline 22 Jan 2015,* The wall street journal

Popkin, M. & Nehal, B. (1999), *Latin American Amnesties in Comparative Perspective: Can the Past Be Buried,* Ethics & International Affairs, Vol. 13

Popkin and Roht-Arriaza (1995), *Truth as Justice: Investigatory Commissions in Latin America,* Law & social inquiry, 20(1)

PRIDE (2002), *Ex-combatant views of Truth and Reconciliation Commission and the Special Court in Sierra Leone,* Freetown: Post-conflict Reintegration Initiative for Development and Empowerment (PRIDE) in partnership with the International Centre for Transitional Justice (ICTJ), retrieved from http://www.ictj.org/sites/default/files/ICTJ-SierraLeone-Combatants-TRC-2002-English.pdf

Pradhan, G. (n.d.), *Nepal's civil war and its economic costs,* Journal of International and Global studies, Eastern Kentucky University

Hayner, P.B. (1994), *Fifteen Truth Commissions -- 1974 to 1994: A Comparative Study,* In Human Rights Quarterly, Vol. 16, Issue: 4. 1994, p. 558

Preucel, R., & Mrozowski, S. (Eds.), (2010), *Contemporary archaeology in theory: The new pragmatism,* Oxford: Willey-Blackwell

Quinn, J. R. (2004), *Constraints: The Un-doing of the Ugandan Truth Commission,* Human Rights Quarterly 26, (2004), pp. 401-427

Ra, S. & Singh, B. (2005), *Nepal: Measuring the Economic Costs of Conflict: The Effect of Declining Development Expenditure,* Kathmandu: Asian Development Bank: Working Paper Series No. 2. Nepal Resident Mission

Rai, D. (2016), *Humane and Rights: Nepal's transitional justice process and human rights,* Kathmandu, retrieved from https://nepalhumanrights. wordpress.com/2016/03/

Ranjitkar, S.B. (2014), *Nepal: Promulgating A New Constitution By February 2015,* retrieved from http://www.scoop.co.nz/stories/HL1404/ S00041/nepal-promulgating-a-new-constitution-by-february-2015. htm

Rees et al (2002), *Colonisation and Conflict 1770-1990,* Oxford: Heinemann Education Publishers

Reno, W. (1995), Corruption and state politics in Sierra Leone, Cambridge: Cambridge University Press

Reno, W. (2003), *Political networks in a failing state: the roots and future of violent conflict in Sierra Leone,* Internationale Politik und Gesellschaft, vol. 2, http://www.fes.de/ipg/IPG2_2003/ARTRENO.HTM

Republica (2017), *Transitional justice mechanisms get one year term extension,* Kathmandu: Republica

Reveron, D. S., & Murer, J. S. (2006), *Flashpoints in the War on Terrorism.* New York: Routledge, Taylor and Francis Group Ltd.

Richards, P. (1996), *Fighting for the rain forest: war, youth & resources in Sierra Leone,* Portsmouth, New Hampshire: Heinemann

Richards P. (1998), *Fighting for the Rainforest. War, Youth and Resources in Sierra Leone,* The International African Institute – James Currey, Oxford: Heinemann

Richards, P. (2003), *The political economy of internal conflict in sierra Leone,* The Netherland: Netherland institute of international relations Clingendael

Ristic, M. (2013), *Serbian Police Accused of Murdering Kosovo Albanians,* Balkan Transitional Justice on 19 June 2013

Rosenberg, T. (1999), *Coming to terms: South Africa's search for truth,* New York: Public Affairs

Rotberg, R. I. (2000), *Truth Commissions and the Provision of Truth, Justice and Reconciliation,* In Rotberg, R. I. & D. Thompson (eds.), *Truth v. Justice: the Morality of Truth Commissions,* (2000) 13.

Rotberg & Thompson, D. (eds.) (2000), *Truth versus Justice: The Morality of Truth Commissions,* Princeton University Press, ISBN 978-0691050720

Rupp, A & E Sorel, (1998*), Economic Models' in National Institute for Mental Health,* on March 1998.

Sajjad, T. (2013), *Transitional justice in south Asia: A study of Afghanistan and Nepal,* London: Routledge

Sapkota, B. (2004), *The Cost of War in Nepal: A Research Study,* Kathmandu: National Peace Campaign (NPC), p. 93

Sarkin & Daly (2001), *Accommodating Individual Criminal Responsibility and National Reconciliation: The UN Truth Commission for East Timor,* American Journal of International Law (2001), pp. 952, 955

Sarkin, J. & E. Daly (2004), *Too Many Questions, Too Few Answers: Reconciliation in Transitional Societies,* 35 Columbia Human Rights Law Review 661, 723

Saunders, C. (2002), *South Africa: recent history,* In Murison, K. (eds), *Africa South of the Sahara,* 965-75, London: Europa

Sawyer, E. & Kelsall, (2007), *Truth vs. Justice? Popular Views on the Truth and Reconciliation Commission and the Special Court for Sierra Leone,* The Online Journal of Conflict Resolution 7(1)

Schalkwyk, D. (2004), *Truth, Reconciliation, and Evil in South Africa,* In Breen, M.S. (ed), *Truth, Reconciliation, and Evil*

Sengupta, S. (2005), *Where maoists still matter,* The New York Times, on October 2005, p.30

Setopati (2015), *News,* Kathmandu, retrieved from setopati.com

Schalkwyk, D. (2004), *Truth, Reconciliation, and Evil in South Africa*, In M. Breen, *Truth, Reconciliation, and Evil* (pp. 3-42), Amsterdam, Netherlands: Rodopi

Shah, A., (2012), *Integration of Maoist combatants in Nepal: The challenges ahead*, New Delhi: ORF, Issue Brief #39

Shahu, M. B. (2013), *Landlessness and land confiscation in Nepal: The context of Maoist insurgency in Nepal*, Contributions of Nepalese studies, CNAS journal, Vol 40, No. 1 (Jan 2013), pp. 61-86, CNAS/TU

Shakya, A. (2006), *Social impact of armed conflict in Nepal: cause and impact*, Kathmandu: SIRF

Shakya, A. (2009), *Social Impact of Armed Conflict in Nepal:Cause and Impact*, Kathmandu: Social inclusion research fund

Sharma, B. (2013), *PR vote count over, NC, UML may get 91, 84 seats*, Kathmandu: Kathmandu Post, retrieved from http://www.ekantipur. com/the-kathmandu-post/2013/11/28/top-story/pr-vote-count-over-nc-uml-may-get-91-84-seats/256286.html Retrieved on 23 Apr,2014

Sharma, S. (2004), *"The Maoist Movement; an Evolutionary Perspective*, In Hutt, M. (2004), (ed.) *Himalayan People's War Nepal's Maoist Rebellion* USA: Indiana University Press

Sharma, K. (2006), *The Political Economy of Civil War in Nepal*, World Development, Vol. 34, No. 7, pp. 1237–1253, 2006 doi:10.1016/j. worlddev.2005.12.001

Shaw, R. (2005), *Rethinking Truth and Reconciliation Commissions: Lessons from Sierra Leone*, United States Institute of Peace, Special Report # 130, on Feb 2005

Shaw, R. (2007), *Memory Frictions: Localizing the Truth and Reconciliation Commission in Sierra Leone*, International Journal of Transitional Justice, 1 (2) 2007, pp. 183-207

Shearer, D. (1997), *Exploring the limits of consent: Conflict resolution in Sierra Leone*, Millennium: Journal of International Studies 26, pp. 845-860

Sheriff, M. & Bobson-Kamara, E.M.J. (2005), *TRC Report: A Secondary School Version,* Truth and Reconciliation Commission Working Group, retrieved from http://www.trcsierraleone.org/pdf/trc_sss.pdf

Sierra Leonean TRC (2003), *Truth and Reconciliation Report for the Children of Sierra Leone: Child-Friendly Version,* retrieved from http://www.trcsierraleone.org/pdf/kids.pdf

Sierra Leonean TRC (2004), *Witness to truth: Report of the Sierra Leone Truth and Reconciliation Commission,* Sierra Leone

Simunovic, I. (2004), *Dealing with the Legacy of Past War Crimes and Human Rights Abuses: Experiences and Trends,* Journal of International Criminal

Singh, S., Dahal, K., Mills, E. (2005), *"Nepal's war on human rights: A summit higher than the Mt. Everest",* International Journal for Equity in Health. Vol. 4, No. 9. DOI: http://dx.doi.org/10.1186/1475-9276-4-9Sola_martin, A. (2009), *Is peacebuildig sustainable in Sierra Leone?,* Global change, Peace & Security, Vol. 21, Iss. 3, 2009

Sooka, Y. (2003), *Apartheid's Victims in the Midst of Amnesty's Promise,* In Charles Villa-Vicencio & Erik Doxtader (eds.) *The Provocations of Amnesty: Memory, Justice and Impunity:*309-314, Claremont: David Philip Publishers

Staff, B. (2010), *Q&A: Sudan's Darfur conflict,* BBC News, 23 Feb 2010, retrieved from www.southasiaanalysis.org

Stanley, E. (2011), *Evaluating the truth and reconciliation commission,* The journal of modern African studies, Vol. 39, No. 3 (Sept. 2001), pp.525-546, Cambridge university press, www.jstor.org/stable/3557322

Steinberg, J. (2009), *Liberia's experiment with transitional justice,* African Affairs, 109/434, 135-144.

Steiner, H. J. (n.d.), *Truth Commissions: A Comparative Assessment,* Harvard Law School., retrieved from http://www.law.harvard.edu/programs/HRP/Publications/truth1.html#anchor1276618

Stewart, P.F. (2012), *Labour time in South Africa gold mines: 1886-2006,* University of the Witwatersrand

Stovel, L. (2006), *Long road home: Building reconciliation and trust in post-war Sierra Leone,* Canada: Simon Fraser University

Subedi, D. B. (2013), *Economic Dimension of Peacebuilding: Insights into post-conflict economic recovery and development in Nepal,* South Asia Economic Journal, 13(2), 313-332

Sudan Tribune Staff (2014, May 26), *Darfur authority appoints justice and reconciliation bodies,* retrieved from Sudan Tribune: Plural news and views on Sudan: 26 May 2014, http://www.sudantribune.com/spip. php?article51127

Suhrke, A. (2009), *An support for peace building: Nepal as the exceptional case,* Norway: Chr. Michelsen Institute

Supreme Court (2007), *Dakhal and Ors. v. Ministry of Home Affairs and Ors.,* Kathmandu: Supreme Court Division Bench, Order of 1 June 2007

Tamang, B.M. (2011), *Nepal's peace process and the International Crisis Group report,* IPCS, retrieved from http://www.ipcs.org/article/south-asia/nepals-peace-process-and-the-icg-report-3429.html

Tamang, B. M. (2011), *Nepal: Disintegration of Madhesi Parties – Analysis,* Institute for Peace and Conflict Studies (IPCS), retrieved from www. eurasiareview.com/10082011-nepal-disintegration-ofmadhesi-parties-analysis

Tamang, B.M. (2013), Nepal's TRC: Can it heal old wounds?, IPCS, retrieved from http://www.ipcs.org/article/nepal/nepals-truth-and-reconciliation-commission-can-it-heal-old-wounds-4125.html

Tamang, L.R. (2012), *Nepal, a constitutional impasse,* Open democracy retrieved from https://www.opendemocracy.net/leena-rikkila-tamang/nepal-constitutional-impasse

Taylor, B.K. (2011), *Sierra Leone: The land, its people and history,* Tanzania: New Africa Press

Thapa, D. (2004), *A Kingdom Under Siege; Nepal's Maoist Insurgency, 1996 to 2004,* Kathmandu: The Print house, pp 48, 53, 71, 72; 211-216

Thapa, D., & Sijapati B. (2006), *A Kingdom under seize: Nepal's Maoist insurgency, 1996 to 2004*, Kathmandu: The Print house

Theissen, G. (1999), *Common Past, Divided Truth: The Truth and Reconciliation Commission in South African Public Opinion*, Spain: International Institute for the Sociology of Law (IISL)

The Himalayan Times (2016), *TRC urges government to solve war-era cases*, News on 7 Feb 2016, retrieved from http://thehimalayantimes.com/ nepal/trc-urges-govt-to-solve-war-era-cases/

The Kathmandu Post (2015), *News: TRC has been formed to restore justice system, reconcile society,* Kathmandu, on 16 Feb 2015, retrieved from http://www.kathmandupost.ekantipur.com/news/2015-02-16/trc-has-been-formed-to-restore-justice-system-reconcile-society.html

The Kathmandu Post (2016), *Sitting on hands awaiting financial leg-up*, Kathmandu, on 12 Feb 2016, retrieved from http://www. kathmandupost.ekantipur.com/news/2016-02-12/sitting-on-hands-awaiting-financial-lef-up.html

The Kathmandu Post (2016), *Local peace committees to be used for collecting complaints*, Kathmandu, on 26 Feb 2016, retrieved from http:// kathmandupost.ekantipur.com/printedition/news/2016-02-26/local-peace-committees-to-be-used-for-collecting-complaints.html

The Kathmandu Post (2016), *CIEDP to start taking plaints from mid-April*, Kathmandu, on 19 March 2016, retrieved from http://www. kathmandupost.ekantipur.com/printedition/news/2016-03-19/ ciedp-to-start-taking-plaints-from-mid-april.html

The Kathmandu Post (2016), *Politics of restructuring*, Kathmandu, on 2 Sept 2016, retrieved from http://www.kathmandupost.ekantipur. com/printedition/news/2016-09-02/politics-of-restructuring.html

The Rising Nepal (2015), *News: Cabinet appoints Gurung as TRC Chairman, Mallik as CIEDP Head,* Kathmandu, on 10 Feb 2015, retrieved from http://www.therisingnepal.org.np/news/1559

Thomas, B. (1994), *The United Nations Truth Commission for El Salvador*, Vanerbilt Journal of Transitional Law, Vol. 27, No. 3 (1994), pp. 497

Thompson, L. (1995), *A History of South Africa*. Binghamton, New York: SUNY Press/New Haven: Yale University Press.

Tina, R. (1995), *Overcoming the Legacies of Dictatorship*, Foreign Affairs, 74, May/June

Tiwari, N. (2014), *Constitution writing: set process Vs Consensus*, Kathmandu: Gorkhapatra National Daily, on 10 Nov. 2014

Torpey, J. C., (ed.), 2003, *Politics and the Past: On Repairing Historical Injustices*, Lanham, MD: Rowman & Littlefield

Totten, C. D. (2009), *The International Criminal Court andTruth Commissions: A Framework for Cross-Interaction in the Sudan and Beyond*, Northwestern Journal of International Human Rights, Vol. 7, No. 1, pp. 1-33.

Transitional Working Group (2008), *Generating recommendations for the Liberian truth and reconciliation commission: Civil society regional consultations*, Report: Transitional justice working group, Catholic justice and peace commission

Transparency International (2006), *New anti-corruption governments: Liberia's challenge to deliver*, Transparency International

TRC Act, (2002), *Ghanian TRC Act*, retrieved from http://www.ghanareview.com/reconact.html

TRC Act (2000), *Sierra Leonean TRC Act*, retrieved from http://www.sierraleone.org/trcact2000.html.

TRC Act (2000), *Sierra Leonean TRC Act*, retrieved from www.sierra-leone.org/Laws/2000-4.pdf

TRC Act (2014), *Nepalese TRC Act*, retrieved from http://trc.gov.np/base/file/actsrulesguidelines.pdf

TRC (1998), *TRC Report, vol 5*, South Africa: Truth and Reconciliation Commission

TRC (2004) *TRC Report*, Sierra Leone: Truth and Reconciliation Commission

TRC (2009) *TRC Report*, Liberia: Truth and Reconciliation Commission

TRC (2016) *TRC Interim Report*, Nepal: Truth and Reconciliation Commission

TRC (2016), *Interaction program with Government officers, civil society, journalists and conflict victims based in various districts*, Kathmandu: Truth and Reconciliation commission

Tutu, D. (1999), *No Future without Forgiveness*, London: Rider Books

UNDP,(2001), *Human development report 2001*, USA: United Nations Development Programme

UNDP (2006), *Case Study Sierra Leone*, USA: United Nations Development Programme

UNDP (2014), *Human development Report-2014*, USA: United Nations Development Programme

UNDP (2015), *Human development Report-2015*, USA: United Nations Development Programme

UNDP (2016), *Human development Report-2016*, USA: United Nations Development Programme

UNHCHR (2006), *Rule-of-law tools for post-conflict states: Truth commissions*, New York and Geneva: United Nations

UNHCR (2005), *From emergency evacuation to community empowerment: Review of the reparation and reintegration programme in Sierra Leone*, Sperl, Geneva: S & De Vriese, M.

United Nations (2006), *Rule-of-law tools for post-conflict states: Truth Commissions*, New York and Geneva: United Nations

United Nations Secretary (2005) *Report of the International Commission of Inquiry on Darfur to the United Nations Secretary-Genera*, Geneva: United Nations

United Nations Staff (2005) *Report of the International Commission of Inquiry on Darfur to the United Nations Secretary-General*, Geneva: United Nations

UN (2001), *Peacebuilding: Towards a comprehensive Approach*, Statement by the President of the Security Council, 20 Feb 2001, United NationsUN (1999), *Security council establishes UN mission for Sierra*

Leone to aid with implementation of Lome Peace agreement, Press release SC/6742, on 22 Oct 1999, United Nations

United Nations Transitional Administration for East Timor (2001), *Truth and Reconciliation in East Timor, Regulation No. 2001/10: On the Establishment of a Commission for Reception,* on 13 July 2001, s21(2)

Upreti, B.R. (2006), *Armed conflict and peace process in Nepal,* India: Adroit Publishers

Upreti, B.R., (2010), *Armed Conflict and Peace Process in Nepal: The Maoist insurgency, past negotiations, and opportunities for conflict transformation,* New Delhi: Adroid Publishers, p. 260

Upreti, B.R. (2011), *Integrating Maoist ex-combatants in Nepal,* South Asia Journal, July-September 2011

USIP (2002), *Truth Commission: Sierra Leone,* USA: United States Institute of Peace, on 1 Nov 2002

USIP (2011), *Truth commission digital collection,* USA: United States Institute of Peace, on 16 March 2011

Vaughn, B. (2006), *Nepal: Background and U.S. Relations,* U.S. Library of Congress, Congressional Research Service

Venhaus, J. M. "Matt" (2010), *Why youth join al- Qaeda?,* USIP Special Report 236, Washington DC: United States Institute for Peace.Verdoolaege, A. & Kerstens, P. (2004), *The South African Truth and Reconciliation Commission and the Belgian Lumumba Commission: A Comparison.* Africa Today 50(3): 75-91

Wain, M. (2003), *Ghana's National Reconciliation Commission: Peace Magaine,* Apr-Jun 2003, p.18, retrieved from http://archive. peacemagazine.org/v19n2p18.htm

Wakugawa, I. at el (ed.) (2011), *From conflict to peace in Nepal: Peace Agreement 2005-2010,* Kathmandu: Asian Study Center for Peace & Conflict Transformation

Walker, M. U. (2006), *Moral Repair: Reconstructing Moral Relations after Wrongdoing,* New York: Cambridge University Press

_____ (2010), *Truth Telling as Reparations*, Metaphilosophy, 41(4): 525–45

Wallton, A. (2014), A Master's dissertation on '*Addressing falsehoods and misconceptions of the past: The Liberian Truth and Reconciliation Commission reinterpreting Liberia's past*', Historiska Institutionen

Warisha, F. W. & Hayner, P. (2009), *The Initiative for Peacebuilding, Negotiating Peace in Nepal: Implications for Justice*, International Centre for Transitional Justice (ICTJ), on 20 June 2009

Weah, A. (2012), *Hopes and Uncertainties: Liberia's Journey to End Impunity*, International Journal of Transitional Justice 6, No. 2 (2012): 331–43

Weaver, A. D. (2016), A Master's thesis on '*Truth and justice? Towards comprehensive transitional justice in Uganda and the democratic republic of Congo* ', Nebraska: The university of Nebraska

Weinstein, J. (2002), *The structure of rebel organizations: Implications for post conflict reconstruction*, Research Dissemination Note 4, Washington DC: Conflict Prevention and Research Unit, The World Bank

Whitfield, T. (2008), *Masala Peacemaking: Nepal's peace process and the contribution of outsiders*, New York

Williams, P.J. (1991), *Alchemy of Race and Rights: Diary of a Law Professor*, Harvard University Press, pp. 146-166

Williams, P. (2001), *Fighting for Freetown: British Military Intervention in Sierra Leone*, Contemporary Security Policy, Vol. 22, No. 3, pp. 140–168

Wilson, M. (1969), *The hunters and herders*, In Wilson, M. & Thompson, L. (eds), *The Oxford history of south Africa*, Oxord, Vol I: South Africa

Wilson, R. (1995), *Manufacturing legitimacy: the TRC and the Rule of Law*, Indicator: South Africa 13, 1: 41-6

WB (2011), *World development report 2011: Conflict, security and development*, Washington D.C.: The World Bank, in Yadav, P. (2016), *Social transformation in Post-conflict Nepal: A gender perspective*, London: Routledge

Zartman, I. W. (1995), *Dynamics and Constraints in Negotiations in Internal Conflicts*, In W. Zartman (ed), *Elusive Peace: Negotiating and End to Civil Wars*, Washington: Brookings Institute, pp. 3-29.

Zehr, H. (1997), *Restorative Justice: When justice and healing go together*, Track Two 6/3&4: 20.

Index

A

African national congress xi

Agreement on Monitoring of the Management of Arms and Armies 30

All People's Congress xi, 80

American colonization society xi

Americo-Liberian rule 61, 68

Amnesty International 27

Amnesty Nepal 25

Anti-corruption Commission xi, 91, 92, 93, 122

Armed Forces Ruling Council xi, 81

Army Integration Special Committee (ASISC) 30

B

Baburam Bhattarai 25

C

Centre for Humanitarian Dialogue and Carter Centre 27

Commission on Enforced Disappearances xi, 1, 173

Commission on Investigation of Disappeared Persons (CIDP) xi, 35

Communist Party of Nepal (Maoist) xi, xiii, 29, 36, 129, 169

Comprehensive Peace Accord viii, xi, 1, 28, 29, 35, 38, 69, 133, 144, 164

Convention on the Elimination of All Forms of Discrimination against Women 9

D

Disarmament, Demobilization and Reintegration xii, 81

Dutch Reformed Church xii, 103

E

Economic Community of West African States xii, 55, 64, 66, 82, 83, 111, 114

Enforced Disappearances 1, 34, 173

H

Human development record xii

I

Improvised Explosive Devices (IEDs) 20, 151